SOME RECORDS

OF THE

DYER FAMILY

COMPILED BY

CORNELIA C. JOY-DYER

"*Remember the days of old, consider the years of many generations: ask thy father, and he will shew thee; thy elders, and they will tell thee.*—DEUTERONOMY xxxii. 7.

"*I have considered the days of old, the years of ancient times.*"—PSALM lxxvii. 5.

PRINTED FOR PRIVATE CIRCULATION

NEW YORK
THOMAS WHITTAKER
2 AND 3 BIBLE HOUSE
1884

To the

Rev. Heman Dyer, D.D.

This History of his Ancestors
is affectionately inscribed
by his Wife

To the

REV. HEMAN DYER, D.D.

THIS HISTORY OF HIS ANCESTORS
IS AFFECTIONATELY INSCRIBED
BY HIS WIFE

PREFACE.

The following pages have not been hastily written, but are the result of much patient, and thoughtful research. Great care has been taken that no statement should be made, without ample proof of its correctness. Numerous books, and musty records, have been consulted, and the most persevering, and untiring efforts made, to reach the truth. If mistakes can be found, it is believed that they are but slight ones. It may be thought that some matters have been introduced, which are foreign to the subject; but in each instance, there has been a motive for doing so. There has been no attempt to trace the lineage of the various branches of the Dyer family. The object of the writer was to find the link between the noble-hearted martyr, Mary Dyre —her brave husband—and that branch of their descendants for which she has a particular regard. It is believed that much of interest will be found, in the book, to any bearing the name, and certainly *all* are justified in feeling both pride and pleasure, who can trace their lineage back to that remarkable band of Exiles, who left their native land for conscience' sake, came to this wilderness, and, after years of trial, toil, and embarrassment, most cheerfully and nobly borne, laid the foundation for the rich inheritance we now enjoy. Such an ancestry is indeed a "precious heritage."

> "Yet, remember! 'tis a crown
> That can hardly be thine own,
> Till thou win it by some deed
> That with glory fresh shall feed
> Their renown!"

CORNELIA C. JOY-DYER.

NEW YORK, March, 1884.

SOME RECORDS OF THE DYER FAMILY.

FIFTEEN years after the Pilgrims of the Mayflower had landed on Plymouth Rock, we find the first record of William and Mary Dyre, in Boston. A family tradition says that two brothers and a sister—Edward, George, and Tabitha Dyre—came from England to Boston in the Mayflower, about 1627 or 1629. With them, were the son of one brother and the daughter of the other—William and Mary. The cousins married; *when*, it is not known. As it has been impossible to ascertain any other maiden name for Mary Dyre, the inference is that the tradition may be a correct one. Gerard Croese in his "History of the Quakers," quaintly describes her as "a person of no mean extract or parentage, of an estate pretty plentiful, of a comely stature and countenance, of a piercing knowledge in many things, of a wonderful sweet and pleasant discourse." Governor John Winthrop, in his Journal dated 1638, speaks of her as "a very *promp*, and fair woman, of a very proud spirit." "Thus," says Drake in his "New England Legends," "we have, in her, the portrait of a comely woman of fine presence, high spirit, a fair share of education, and possessing, moreover, a soul endowed with the purpose of an evangelist, or, at need, a martyr." The Dyre family, like many others in that day, had left the refinements of an English home, and braved the discomforts of the western wilderness, in order to enjoy the blessings of religious liberty. William and Mary Dyre united with the church of which the Rev. Mr. Wilson, (afterwards so malignant in his persecution of the Quakers) was the pastor, and on the 20th of December, 1635, their son Samuel was baptized. The following March, William Dyre was made freeman. As this act gave him the elective franchise, and was not bestowed without a certain amount of property, it is probable that he was a man of some means, when this privilege was conferred upon him. The name Dyre has, like many names in this country, been spelled in various ways by different branches of the family. We find it thus written— Dier, Dhier, Dyor, Dyar, Dyre and Dyer,—the last being the spelling by which the name is now known, both in England and America. William, of Boston, wrote his name Dyre, as his ancestors had done for many years, and thus it continued for several generations in this country. In Anglo-Saxon the adjective *dyre* means "strong—bold." In the days of Chaucer, *dyre* meant "dear," and he says:

"Farewelle, *dyre* herte, chef yn remembraunce,
And ever schalle unto the oure y dy."

It is not known how much the ancestors of William

Dyre were governed by these considerations in spelling their names, but the Anglo-Saxon meaning probably had its influence. About the time that the Dyre family came among the Puritans of New England, Roger Williams, originally from Wales, and a graduate of Pembroke College, Cambridge, then a young man of thirty-two years of age, had made his appearance, and taken a decided stand against many of the views of the founders of Massachusetts, who came to secure freedom for the exercise of their own religious opinions, but were zealous in putting down all those who differed from them. He believed in religious freedom, not only for his own opinions, but for those of all others. He thought that the law ought to be used to keep people from crime, but that it had nothing to do with their religious belief. He did not approve of obliging people to attend church, unless they wished to do it. He did not think it right to choose the magistrates from the church members only, or to make people pay to support the church unless they wished. There were many who shared these views, but had not the courage to avow them, knowing it might bring them into serious difficulties. Petitions, however, were gotten up, protesting against these requirements, and agents were sent about to get signers. They soon got into trouble, and one incident will show how bitter was the feeling against them. My ancestor, Thomas Joy, in an unwary moment, was persuaded to carry a petition for signatures. John Winthrop, Esq., first Governor of the colony of Massachusetts Bay, makes this record in his

Journal: "There was, also, one Thomas Joy, a young fellow, whom they had employed to get hands for the petition. He began to be very busy, but was laid hold on and kept in irons about four or five days, and then he humbled himself, confessed what he knew, and blamed himself for meddling in matters belonging not to him, and blessed God for these irons upon his legs, hoping they would *do him good*, while he lived! So he was let out upon reasonable bail."

A novel way of taking iron as a tonic!

Roger Williams talked so boldly against the established laws, that the Massachusetts magistrates decided to send him back to England. He heard of this intention and fled, in mid winter, from his home in Salem, and wandered in the wilderness for fourteen weeks, "sorely tost in a bitter season," he says, "not knowing what bread or bed did mean."

This was in January, 1636. It has been shrewdly said that, "when the Pilgrims landed on Plymouth Rock they fell upon their knees, and shortly after, fell upon the aborigines." Roger Williams, however, pursued a different course. He sought the friendship of the Indians, and by kindness and attention, making them presents, and visiting them, as his letters describe, "in their filthy, smoky holes, to gain their tongue," he overcame the shyness of old Canonicus, and won the esteem of the high-spirited Miantinomo. It proved well for himself, and for New England, that this intercourse was maintained. He crossed the Narragansett Bay, with five companions, in an Indian

Dyre were governed by these considerations in spelling their names, but the Anglo-Saxon meaning probably had its influence. About the time that the Dyre family came among the Puritans of New England, Roger Williams, originally from Wales, and a graduate of Pembroke College, Cambridge, then a young man of thirty-two years of age, had made his appearance, and taken a decided stand against many of the views of the founders of Massachusetts, who came to secure freedom for the exercise of their own religious opinions, but were zealous in putting down all those who differed from them. He believed in religious freedom, not only for his own opinions, but for those of all others. He thought that the law ought to be used to keep people from crime, but that it had nothing to do with their religious belief. He did not approve of obliging people to attend church, unless they wished to do it. He did not think it right to choose the magistrates from the church members only, or to make people pay to support the church unless they wished. There were many who shared these views, but had not the courage to avow them, knowing it might bring them into serious difficulties. Petitions, however, were gotten up, protesting against these requirements, and agents were sent about to get signers. They soon got into trouble, and one incident will show how bitter was the feeling against them. My ancestor, Thomas Joy, in an unwary moment, was persuaded to carry a petition for signatures. John Winthrop, Esq., first Governor of the colony of Massachusetts Bay, makes this record in his

Journal: "There was, also, one Thomas Joy, a young fellow, whom they had employed to get hands for the petition. He began to be very busy, but was laid hold on and kept in irons about four or five days, and then he humbled himself, confessed what he knew, and blamed himself for meddling in matters belonging not to him, and blessed God for these irons upon his legs, hoping they would *do him good*, while he lived! So he was let out upon reasonable bail."

A novel way of taking iron as a tonic!

Roger Williams talked so boldly against the established laws, that the Massachusetts magistrates decided to send him back to England. He heard of this intention and fled, in mid winter, from his home in Salem, and wandered in the wilderness for fourteen weeks, "sorely tost in a bitter season," he says, "not knowing what bread or bed did mean."

This was in January, 1636. It has been shrewdly said that, "when the Pilgrims landed on Plymouth Rock they fell upon their knees, and shortly after, fell upon the aborigines." Roger Williams, however, pursued a different course. He sought the friendship of the Indians, and by kindness and attention, making them presents, and visiting them, as his letters describe, "in their filthy, smoky holes, to gain their tongue," he overcame the shyness of old Canonicus, and won the esteem of the high-spirited Miantinomo. It proved well for himself, and for New England, that this intercourse was maintained. He crossed the Narragansett Bay, with five companions, in an Indian canoe, and the first place where he landed, he called Providence, thus acknowledging his gratitude to God. There were no white settlers in that region; and Canonicus and Miantinomo were sachems over the Narragansetts, and resided on the island of Canonicut in the Narragansett Bay. It was from them that Mr. Williams obtained his first deed of the lands about Providence. This deed bears date March 24, 1637, and it mentions a sale of lands to him, and a large tract of country, which, " in consideration of the many kindnesses and services he hath continually done for us, we doe freely give unto him." " It was not price and money," says Roger Williams, " that could have purchased Rhode Island, but it was obtained by love." But he kept nothing himself; he gave away his lands to those he thought most in want, and only desired that a shelter might be found for " persons distressed for conscience." Many such came in process of time; for the " Antinomian controversy," as it was called, had caused great disturbance in Boston. The leaders of it, the Rev. John Wheelwright, and his sister-in-law, Mrs. Ann Hutchinson, promulgated their views so freely that they were banished from the colony—the former going to the head-waters of the Piscataqua, and the latter following Roger Williams.

William Dyre had not remained a silent spectator in all this controversy. He warmly espoused the cause of Wheelwright; and to use his own words, " because his hand was to the seditious writing and *defended the same*," he was disfranchised and disarmed, and finally was driven out of Massachusetts Colony, to the new settlement formed by Roger Williams. Mary Dyre had taken a prominent part in the Antinomian controversy, whilst her force of character, and vigorous understanding, no doubt, caused her to be regarded as a formidable opponent by the orthodox Puritans. When Mrs. Hutchinson was cast out of the church, young Mrs. Dyre walked out with her, in presence of the whole congregation. A fact recorded by Governor Winthrop.

The brave woman, even then, was not afraid to "show her colors."

Soon after reaching their new home, *William Dyre* joined seventeen others, and they bought the island of Rhode Island, then called Aquidneck, or the "Isle of Peace,"—a name which should have been retained, but Governor Coddington thought otherwise, and, from a fancied resemblance to the Isle of Rhodes in the Mediterranean Sea, he changed the name, and it soon became known as Rhode Island. Pocasset was the Indian name of the place where the first English settlement upon Aquidneck was established. Ten coats, and twenty hoes, were given to the resident Indians to vacate the lands, and five fathoms of wampum were paid to the local sachem. Before leaving Providence, this civil compact was drawn up and signed:

"7th day of the 1st month (March), 1638.

"We, whose names are underwritten, do hereby solemnly, in the presence of Jehovah, incorporate ourselves into a body politic; and as he shall help, will submit our persons, lives, and estates unto our Lord Jesus Christ, the King of Kings and Lord of Lords, and to all those perfect and most absolute laws of His, given us in His holy word of truth, to be guided and judged thereby.

"Exodus, xxiv. 3, 4. II. Chron. xi. 3. II. Kings, xi. 17."

Its signers were William Coddington, John Clarke, William Hutchinson, John Coggeshall, Wm. Aspinwall, Samuel Wilbore, John Porter, John Sanford, Edward Hutchinson, Jr., Thomas Savage, *William Dyre*, William Freeborne, Philip Shearman, John Walker, Richard Carder, Wm. Baulstone, Edward Hutchinson, Sr., Henry Bull. The names of Roger Williams and Randall Holden appear as witnesses. On that day, *William Dyre* was chosen the first clerk of the colony. He was also chosen clerk when Newport was settled in 1639. Upon consolidation of the towns into "Providence Plantation in Narragansett Bay in New England" in 1647, he was General Recorder; in 1648, he was Clerk of Assembly; and in 1650, Attorney-General. These official positions show the high estimation in which he was evidently held. A year after the settlement at Pocasset, the colony had increased so greatly, that a division was deemed expedient. A meeting was held, at which the following agreement was entered into by the signers, by whom the settlement of Newport was commenced on the southwest side of the island:

"Pocasset on the 28th of the 2d, 1639.

"It is agreed by us, whose hands are underwritten, to propagate a plantation in the midst of the island or elsewhere; and doe engage ourselves to bear equall charges, answerable to our strength and estates in common; and that our determination shall be by major voice of judge and elders, the judge to have a double voice."

Present:

William Coddington, Judge.

Nicholas Caston, John Coggeshall, Wm. Breton, John Clarke, Jeremy Clerke, Thomas Hazard, Henry Bull, Elders.

William Dyre, Clerk.

In "Extracts from Rhode Island Colonial Records, papers never before published, relating to the original grant of lands to the early settlers of Newport, R. I.," it is stated that "William Dyre having exhibited his bill under the Treasurer's hand unto the sessions held on the 10th of March, 1640, wherein appears full satisfaction to be given for seventy-five acres of land, lying within the precincts of such bounds, as by the committee, by order appointed, did bound it withal, viz.: To begin at the river's mouth, over against Coaster's Harbour, and so by the sea, to run up to a marked stake, at Mr. Coddington's corner, and so down, upon an easterly line to a marked tree over against the Great Swamp, and so two rods within the swamp, at the two deepest corners of the clear land, the one at the southeast corner, and the other upon a straight line in the northeast, marked by stakes, and so down to a marked tree by the river side; the river being his bounds to the mouth thereof, with a home lot and a parcel of meadow and upland lying between Mr. Jeremy Clarke's meadow, and Mr. Jeoffrey's at the north end of the harbour, and north upon the highway, with ten acres allowed by the town order for his travelling about the island, lying within the former bounds, which is his proportion.

"This, therefore, doth evidence and testify, that all those parcels of land before specified, amounting to the number of eighty-seven acres, more or less, is fully impropriated to said William Dyre and his heirs for ever."

This land is beautifully situated on Narragansett Bay, opposite Coaster's Island, and is at the extreme end of what is called "Old Newport." When I visited the place in September, 1883, I found an old family burial ground of the Dyres, which is protected by a high, strong fence, and is literally "impropriated to the heirs of William Dyre, *forever*." It was very touching to look upon this "God's acre," the only relic left to show who were the proprietors of that lovely spot, more than two centuries ago.

With Longfellow,

"I like that ancient Saxon phrase which calls
The burial ground God's acre! It is just.
It consecrates each grave within its walls,
And breathes a benison o'er the sleeping dust."

Many of the inscriptions on the tombstones are legible, but undoubtedly, many stones have been broken, and destroyed, by the ravages of time. It is probable, also, that there were some interments, with no stones to mark the last resting place of those who were buried there. The oldest stone legible is that of Desire Dyre, 1707, and the last interment was that of Wm. Dyre of South Kingstown, September, 1797, aged 91 years. Besides this estate and some other lands, *William Dyre* of Newport, owned an island in Narragansett Bay containing 600 acres which was called "Dyre's Island," and still bears his name. On the 5th August, 1670, he gave it to his son William. After the settlement of Rhode Island, many people of various opinions went there, and it used to be said that any man who had lost his religion would be sure to find it again, at some village in Rhode Island! "The laws of the colony were based on the plan of perfect religious toleration, and good Roger Williams would not permit any thing else. In the mean time, there were various organizations for the protection of the laws. A formal act of the whole people passed at this time, will set their regard for justice and their care in providing for its administration, in still clearer light.

"By the Body Politicke in the Isle of Aquitteneck, inhabiting this present 25th of 9th month, 1639.

"In the fourteenth yeare of y⁵ Raign of our Soveraign Lord, King Charles. It is agreed, that as natural subjects to our Prince, and subject to his Lawes, all matters that concerne the Peace shall be by those that are officers straight line in the northeast, marked by stakes, and so down to a marked tree by the river side; the river being his bounds to the mouth thereof, with a home lot and a parcel of meadow and upland lying between Mr. Jeremy Clarke's meadow, and Mr. Jeoffrey's at the north end of the harbour, and north upon the highway, with ten acres allowed by the town order for his travelling about the island, lying within the former bounds, which is his proportion.

"This, therefore, doth evidence and testify, that all those parcels of land before specified, amounting to the number of eighty-seven acres, more or less, is fully impropriated to said William Dyre and his heirs for ever."

This land is beautifully situated on Narragansett Bay, opposite Coaster's Island, and is at the extreme end of what is called "Old Newport." When I visited the place in September, 1883, I found an old family burial ground of the Dyres, which is protected by a high, strong fence, and is literally "impropriated to the heirs of William Dyre, *forever*." It was very touching to look upon this "God's acre," the only relic left to show who were the proprietors of that lovely spot, more than two centuries ago.

With Longfellow,

"I like that ancient Saxon phrase which calls
The burial ground God's acre! It is just.
It consecrates each grave within its walls,
And breathes a benison o'er the sleeping dust."

Many of the inscriptions on the tombstones are legible, but undoubtedly, many stones have been broken, and destroyed, by the ravages of time. It is probable, also, that there were some interments, with no stones to mark the last resting place of those who were buried there. The oldest stone legible is that of Desire Dyre, 1707, and the last interment was that of Wm. Dyre of South Kingstown, September, 1797, aged 91 years. Besides this estate and some other lands, *William Dyre* of Newport, owned an island in Narragansett Bay containing 600 acres which was called "Dyre's Island," and still bears his name. On the 5th August, 1670, he gave it to his son William. After the settlement of Rhode Island, many people of various opinions went there, and it used to be said that any man who had lost his religion would be sure to find it again, at some village in Rhode Island! "The laws of the colony were based on the plan of perfect religious toleration, and good Roger Williams would not permit any thing else. In the mean time, there were various organizations for the protection of the laws. A formal act of the whole people passed at this time, will set their regard for justice and their care in providing for its administration, in still clearer light.

"By the Body Politicke in the Isle of Aquitteneck, inhabiting this present 25th of 9th month, 1639.

"In the fourteenth yeare of ye Raign of our Soveraign Lord, King Charles. It is agreed, that as natural subjects to our Prince, and subject to his Lawes, all matters that concerne the Peace shall be by those that are officers of the Peace transacted ; And all actions of the case, on Debt, shall be in such Courts as by order are here appointed and, by such Judges as are deputed, heard and legally determined.

"Given at Niew-Port on the Quarter Courte day which was adjourned till ye day.

"*William Dyre*, Secretary."

At the first General Court of Election ever held in Newport, in 1640, various officers were elected; among them, William Coddington Governor, *William Dyre* Secretary.

The first General Assembly met at Portsmouth, 1647, when William Dyre was chosen Recorder. They agreed upon a body of laws, chiefly taken from the laws of England, with the addition of a few suited to their particular circumstances. The code, which contains nothing except civil regulations, concludes thus: "Otherwise than thus, what is herein forbidden, all men may walk as their consciences persuade them, every one in the name of his God. And let the lambs of the Most High walk, in this colony, without molestation, in the name of Jehovah, their God, for ever and ever."

Governor Coddington, it is said, was "among the most turbulent spirits." He was strongly attached to the King's party, against that of the Protector, and maintained that his authority was paramount in the government of the colony. In 1649, Coddington went to England, and found King Charles already beheaded, and the Commonwealth declared. He obtained a hearing of the

Council, and received a commission to govern the island of Rhode Island, and Canonicut, during his life, with a council of six men, to be named by the people and approved by himself. The alarm felt throughout the colony was great, and preparations were immediately made to send delegates to England, to obtain a revocation of Coddington's power. John Clarke, Roger Williams, and William Dyre were sent, and accomplished their important errand. An order of council was issued, vacating the commission of Coddington, and ordering the towns again to unite under the charter. The mission was successful, at every point. Two of the agents remained in England, on their private business, and also to sustain the rights of the colony, while *William Dyre* returned home with the joyful news, leaving his wife, who had accompanied him, in England. This was in 1652. Some time afterward, when Coddington was elected Commissioner, and there was great dissatisfaction, he was compelled to submit to the authority of the colony in these words: " I, William Coddington, do hereby submit to ye authoritie of His Highness in this Colonie, as it is now united, and that, with all my heart." In 1653, active measures were taken against the Dutch, who were sending exploring parties, and making claims along Long Island Sound. *William Dyre* received a commission to act against the enemy, and for a time commanded a privateer. The commission " constituted Captain John Underhill Commander-in-Chief upon the land, and *Captain William Dyre* Commander-in-Chief at sea; yet "to join in counsel, to be assistant each to the other, for the propagating of the service promised." How much maritime skill William Dyre possessed has not come down to us, but he seems to have been ready for any emergency. His dislike of Coddington continued all these years, and there seemed little probability of any harmony between them. In an article on "Highways," from the Colonial Land Evidence, he speaks of a "highway from the town, laid out, of two poles wide, to William Dyre's farm, and so to lead to the lands on the north side of the town, viz.: the meadows, Mr. Coddington's cow pasture, the Artillery garden, etc." He significantly adds, "Thus much I have said and do affirm to the best of my understanding and knowledge, in the common good, wherein all men have right, and if any one is impeached the whole is wronged (as to concerning highways through which all have propriety of free egress). And because this particular doth emearge to that which is committed to our care, I do declare, in my observation, two or three impediments: First, Mr. Coddington, in that highway that goes to the Artillery garden and burying place, he hath set near sixty poles of fencing upon the highway, six feet at least, at the north end. Let them, therefore, that know any injury in this kind, put it down, under their hands, as I now have done, and be ready to make it good, as I am, so shall we avoid hypocrisy, dissimulation, back-bitting, and secret wolveish devourings, one of another, and declare ourselves men, which, how unmanlike the practice of some sycovents are, is and may safely be demonstrated: Therefore, let all that love the light come forth to the light and show their deeds. So saith *William Dyre.* This as a record, I give forth to be a record, from the simple and honest intent of my heart and soul, this 15th February, 1654."

Certainly no one can accuse William Dyre of a want of frankness, and he seems always to have been most honorable in his intention, and just in his dealings. His dislike of Governor Coddington was always ready to manifest itself. This dislike was shared by many others, and a letter was addressed to Oliver Cromwell, setting forth the complaints of the colonists, to which he replied by letter March 29th, 1655, telling them that they were to "proceed in their government according to the tenor of their charter, taking care of the peace and safety of those plantations, that neither through any intestine commotions, or foreign invasions, there do arise any detriment or dishonor to this commonwealth." He adds, "And so we bid you farewell, and rest your loving friend, OLIVER, P."

As their "loving friend" did not long remain Protector, a very liberal charter was granted by King Charles II., July 8, 1663, and remained in force for many years. In 1664, the royal commissioners having nearly completed the subjugation of the Dutch provinces, had their headquarters on board the English fleet lying in the harbor of New York. A delegation, consisting of John Clarke, who had lately returned home, Captain John Cranston, and *Wm. Dyre,* was sent on with a letter from the authorities of Rhode Island, expressing the gratitude of the colony to his Majesty for the charter, and congratulating the commissioners. It is pleasant to know that, after various litigations with Coddington for many years, William Dyre and he were formally reconciled to each other May 14, 1656.

But a great sorrow was in store for *William Dyre.* When he left England in 1652, his wife remained there with her relatives. One can imagine her delight in seeing once more the beautiful land of her birth, after all the hardships of this western wilderness. During her visit of five years in Great Britain, Mary Dyre became a Friend, and was a minister of that society, at the time of her return to the forbidden port of Boston. The year 1656 will be darkly memorable in the annals of New England, for the arrival of the Quakers, and the commencement of their persecution in Boston. The appearance of this "cursed sect of heretics," as they were called, so alarmed the Puritans, that a day of public humiliation was appointed to be held in all the churches, mainly on their account. A stringent law was enacted for their suppression, and two years later, their tenets were made a capital offence. Fines, imprisonment, whipping, banishment, mutilation, and death, were inflicted upon them.

The wildest fanaticism on the part of the Quakers was met by frenzied bigotry on the part of the Puritans. Such was the most miserable state of affairs, when Mary Dyre, in 1657, returned to the land of her adoption. She had no knowledge of what had been done in Massachusetts, but was at once seized, and cast into prison.

When her husband (who had not adopted the faith of the Friends) heard of her imprisonment, he came from Rhode Island, and succeeded in obtaining her release, and leave to take her home, after becoming "bound in a great penalty not to lodge her in any town of the colony, nor to permit any to have speech with her on the journey."

What a meeting for the long-parted husband and wife, and how humiliating such a concession! Mary Dyre spent some time in her Newport home, and then ventured again into Massachusetts, to carry comfort and cheer, to her captive fellow-believers there, feeling that she went in obedience to the divine call. She was again imprisoned, and at her arraignment before Governor Endicott she "gave no other answer but that she denied our law, and came to bear witness against it, and could not choose but come."

One cannot but think, in this connection, of the often quoted saying of grand old Martin Luther, when he made his defence at the Diet of Worms. "Here stand I. *I can do no otherwise.* God help me!" As Mary Dyre's brave determination could not be conquered, Governor Endicott pronounced the sentence of death upon her.

"After Mary Dyer had heard her sentence, she only replied by the significant words, 'The will of the Lord be done.' And when Endicott impatiently exclaimed, 'Take her away, marshal,' she added, 'Yea, joyfully I

go;' for her heart was filled with heavenly consolation from the love of Christ, and from the thought that she was counted worthy to suffer for His sake. She told the marshal that it was unnecessary for him to guard her to the prison. 'I believe you, Mrs. Dyre,' he answered, 'but I must do as I am commanded.' From her prison she addressed an 'Appeal to the Rulers of Boston,' in which she asks nothing for herself, but manifests the courage of an apostle contending for the truth, and the tenderness of a woman, feeling for the sufferings of her people. Her appeal is pervaded throughout, by a simple and touching dignity. She writes: 'Whereas, I am by many charged with the guiltiness of my own blood; if you mean in my coming to Boston, I am therein clear and justified by the Lord, in whose will I came, who will require my blood of you, be sure, who have made a law to take away the lives of the innocent servants of God, if they come among you, who are called by you cursed Quakers; although I say I am a living witness for them and the Lord, that he hath blessed them, and sent them unto you: therefore, be not found fighters against God, but let my counsel and request be accepted with you to repeal all such laws, that the truth and servants of the Lord may have free passage among you, and you be kept frling innocent blood, which I know there are
 you would not do, if they knew it so to
o self ends, the Lord knoweth: for if my
y granted by you it would not avail me,

nor could I expect it of you, so long as I should daily hear or see the sufferings of these people, my dear brethren, with whom my life is bound up, as I have done these two years; and now it is like to increase, even unto death, for no evil doing but coming among you. Was ever the like laws heard of among a people that profess Christ come in the flesh? And have such no other weapons but such laws to fight against spiritual wickedness, withal, as you call it? Woe is me for you! I leave these lines with you, appealing to the faithful and true witness of God, which is one in all consciences, before whom we must all appear—with whom I shall eternally rest in everlasting joy and peace, whether you will hear or forbear. With Him is my reward, with whom to live is my joy, and to die is my gain, though I had not had your forty-eight hours' warning for the preparation of the death of Mary Dyre. Oh, let none of you put this good day far from you, which verily, in the light of the Lord, I see approaching, even to many in and about Boston, which is the bitterest and darkest professing place, and so to continue so long as you have done, that ever I heard of. Let the time past, therefore, suffice for such a profession as brings forth such fruits as these laws are. In love and in the spirit of meekness, I again beseech you, for I have no enmity to the persons of any; but you shall know that God will not be mocked; but what ye sow, that shall ye reap for Him, that will render to every one according to the deeds done in the body, whether good or evil. Even so be it, saith Mary Dyre.'"

It is said that on the day preceding that appointed for the execution, Mary Dyre's eldest son (Samuel) arrived in Boston, and was allowed to remain all night with his mother; he came in the vain hope of inducing her to make such concessions as might be the means of saving her life. Boston Common was separated by the distance of a mile from the jail, and the prisoners were escorted by two hundred men, armed with halberds, guns, swords, and pikes, in addition to many horsemen. The drummers were ordered to walk immediately before the captives, and to beat more loudly, if they should attempt to speak. William Robinson and Marmaduke Stevenson, who had experienced the blessedness of living under a higher and holier law than any mere human authority, felt that the Lord still had need of them to testify for him in this colony, and had remained there, at the peril of their lives. They also were condemned to death, and went with Mary Dyre to the scaffold, "with great cheerfulness," saying "We suffer not as evil-doers, but as those who have testified and manifested the truth." From "A History of the Christian People called Quakers," by William Sewel, I quote the conclusion of this terrible tragedy. "Mary Dyre, seeing her companions hanging dead before her, also stepped up the ladder; but, after her dress was tied about her feet, the noose put about her neck, and her face covered with a handkerchief, which the priest Wilson lent the hangman, just as she was about to be executed, a cry was heard: 'Stop! she is reprieved!' Her feet then being loosed, they bade her come down.

But she, whose mind was already, as it were, in Heaven, stood still, and said she was then willing to suffer as her brethren did, unless they would annul their wicked law. Little heed was given to what she said; but they took her down, and the marshal and others, taking her by the arms, carried her to prison again. That she was freed from the gallows, this time, was at the intercession of her son, to whom, it seems, they could not then resolve to deny that favor. She, now having heard why she was reprieved, wrote the next day, being the 28th of October, 1659, the following letter to the Court:

"'Once more to the General Court assembled in Boston, speaks Mary Dyre, even as before. My life is not accepted, neither availeth me, in comparison of the lives, and liberty of the truth, and servants of the living God, for which, in the bowels of love and meekness, I sought you; yet nevertheless, with wicked hands, have you put two of them to death, which makes me to feel that the mercy of the wicked is cruelty. I rather choose to die than to live, as from you, as guilty of their innocent blood; therefore, seeing my request is hindered, I leave you to the righteous Judge and Searcher of all hearts, who, with the pure measure of light He hath given to every man to profit withal, will, in his due time, let you see whose servants you are, and of whom you have taken counsel, which I desire you to search into, but all his counsel hath been slighted, and you would none of his reproofs. Read your portion: Proverbs, i. 24 to 32.

"'When I heard your last order read, it was a disturbance unto me that was so freely offering up my life to Him that gave it to me, and sent me hither so to do, which obedience he gloriously accompanied with his presence, and peace and love in me, in which I rested from my labors till, by your order and the people. I was so far disturbed that I could not retain any more of the words thereof, than that I should return to prison and there remain forty and eight hours; to which I submitted, finding nothing from the Lord to the contrary, that I may know what His pleasure and counsel is concerning me, on whom I wait therefore, for he is my life and the length of my days; and, as I said before, I came at His command, and go at His command.

" 'Mary Dyre.'

"The magistrates, now perceiving that the putting William Robinson and Marmaduke Stevenson to death caused great discontent among the people, resolved to send away Mary Dyre, thereby to calm their minds a little. And so she was put on horseback, and by four horsemen conveyed fifteen miles towards Rhode Island, where she was left with a horse, and a man, to be conveyed the rest of the way; which she soon sent back, and so repaired home. By the style of her letters and her undaunted carriage, it appears that she had indeed many extraordinary qualities. She was also of a comely and grave countenance, of a good family and estate, and a mother of several children; but her husband, it seems, was of another persuasion.

"After her return to Rhode Island, she went from

thence to Long Island, where she spent the most part of the winter, and then, coming home again, she was moved to return to that bloody town of Boston, whither she came on the 21st of the third month, 1660, and on the 31st she was sent for by the General Court. Being come, the Governor, John Endicott, said: 'Are you the same Mary Dyre that was here before?' And it seems he was preparing an *evasion* for her, as she might easily have replied 'No.' But she was so far from disguising, that she answered, undauntedly: 'I *am* the same Mary Dyre that was here at the last General Court.' Then Endicott said: 'You will own yourself a Quaker, will you not?' To which Mary Dyre said, 'I own myself to be reproachfully called so.' And Endicott said the sentence was passed upon her at the last General Court, and now, likewise. 'You must return to the prison, and there remain till to-morrow, at nine o'clock; then from thence you must go to the gallows, and there be hanged till you are dead.' To which Mary Dyre said: 'This is no more than what thou saidst before.' And Endicott returned: 'But now it is to be executed; therefore, prepare yourself; to-morrow, at nine o'clock.' She then spoke thus: 'I came in obedience to the will of God, the last General Court, desiring you to repeal your unrighteous laws of banishment on pain of death; and that same is my work now, and earnest request; although I told you that, if you refused to repeal them, the Lord would send others of his servants to witness against them.' Whereupon Endicott asked her if she was a prophetess? And she answered that she spoke the words that the Lord spoke in her, and now the thing was come to pass. And beginning to speak of her call, Endicott cried, 'Away with her! away with her!' So she was brought to the prison-house where she was before, and kept close shut up until the next day. About the appointed time the marshal, Michaelson, came, and called her to come hastily; and coming into the room where she was, she desired him to 'stay a little;' and, speaking mildly, said she 'should be ready presently.' But he, being of a rough temper, said he 'could not wait upon her, but she should now wait upon him.' One Margaret Smith, her companion, being grieved to see such hard-heartedness, spoke something against their unjust laws and proceedings. To which he said, 'You shall have your share of the same.' Then Mary Dyre was brought forth, and, with a band of soldiers, led through the town, the drums being beaten before and behind her, and so continued, that none might hear her speak all the way to the place of execution; which was about a mile. With this guard she came to the gallows. and, being gone up the ladder, some said to her that, if she would return, she might come down and save her life. To which she replied, 'Nay, I cannot; for, in obedience to the will of the Lord I came, and in His will I abide, faithful to the death.' Then Captain John Webb said, that she had been there before, and had the sentence of banishment upon pain of death, and broken the law in coming again now, and therefore she was guilty of her own blood. To which she returned: 'Nay, I came to keep blood-guiltiness from you, desiring you to repeal the unrighteous and unjust law of banishment upon pain of death made against the innocent servants of the Lord; therefore, my blood will be required at your hands, who wilfully do it. But for those that do it in the simplicity of their hearts, I desire the Lord to forgive them. I came to do the will of my Father, and in obedience to His will I stand, even to death.' The priest, Wilson, said: 'Mary Dyre, O repent! O repent! and be not so deluded and carried away by the deceit of the devil.' To this Mary Dyre answered: 'Nay, man, I am not now to repent.' And being asked by some, whether she would have the elders pray for her, she said: 'I know never an elder here.' Being farther asked whether she would have any of the people to pray for her, she answered that she desired the prayers of *all* the people of God. When accused of having said she had been in Paradise, she replied without hesitation: 'Yea, I have been in Paradise these several days. This is to me an hour of the greatest joy I ever had in this world. No ear can hear, no tongue can utter, no heart can understand the sweet incomes and the refreshings of the Spirit of the Lord which I now feel!' In this frame of mind, this honest, valiant woman died,—a martyr to her faith."

A Friend who had united in her ministerial services on Shelter Island, sums up his description of her, by saying: "She even shined in the image of God." There will always be a difference of opinion as to the course she pursued; but no one can question her wonderful bravery, and certainly, not many can now be found, who would have the courage to imitate it. The motto of one branch of the Dyer family, "Terrere nolo, timere nescio" (To affright, I would not—*to fear, I know not*), seems to have been applicable in her case. A strong sense of duty, and an intense hatred of wrong, influenced her actions; and while we may, perhaps, feel that it was a mistaken duty, we cannot but admire and reverence the real nobleness, and grandeur, of her character. The "Divine immanence," of which our Quaker poet, John G. Whittier, speaks, seems to have lifted her above all the sufferings of earth, and given her a faith which nothing could weaken—a courage which never faltered.

Edward Wanton, a member of one of the most distinguished families of Rhode Island, and the first of the name in America, was an officer of the guard, when Mary Dyre suffered death. The unshaken firmness with which she submitted to her fate moved Wanton, greatly. "Alas, mother!" said he, as he went into his house after the execution, "we have been murdering the Lord's people;" and taking off his sword, he made a solemn vow never to wear it again. Not long afterward, he became a member of the society of Friends. Amelia Opie, in her excellent work entitled "Illustrations of Lying," mentions Mary Dyre as one of the instances of those whom even the fear of death has not been able to terrify into falsehood, because they were supported in their integrity by the fear of God.

As William Dyre had not adopted the tenets of the

Friends, it could hardly have been possible for him to sympathize in the views of his wife; and no doubt, her course did not always meet with his approval. He wrote many pathetic letters to Governor Endicott, sometimes "blaming her," but speaking of her as his "dear wife." She spent much time away from home, in ministering to the comfort of those who needed her aid. It has been said that "no Puritanical power, no human hand, was strong enough to suppress the heaven-implanted and divinely directed zeal of the Friends to share their spiritual treasure with others." A few days before Mary Dyre's death, her husband in great anguish of mind, he being wholly ignorant that she meditated this fatal step, wrote to the General Court of Massachusetts, once more imploring its clemency. His entreaties would have moved a stone to pity.

But it was now, too late. In a letter to Governor Endicott dated May 27, 1660, he says, "I have not seen my wife lately and, therefore, cannot tell how, in the frame of her spirit, she was moved thus again, to run so great a hazard to herself, and come to your jurisdiction. Unhappy journey!"

Those were, indeed, bitter days for William Dyre, and for his family. There were many other instances of most revolting cruelty practiced upon persons not resident in Rhode Island, and which continued till Charles II. peremptorily forbade any further murders to be perpetrated in the name of God, by those infuriated zealots. An English writer has said that "the most important fact concerning Mary Dyre is that of her murder having been the *motive* of the wonderfully liberal charter granted by Charles II., to the province of Rhode Island, making it the first spot of earth on the globe, whereon religious toleration and absolute freedom of worship were established by law. What influence the Dyres may have possessed at court is not known, but it is possible to account for the interest taken in her fate by Charles II., (who is not to be credited with any purely *humane* considerations,) from the fact that Mary had probably descended from Sir Ludovick Dyer, Baronet, of Stoughton, Hampshire county, whose patent bears date of 8th June, 1627, (temp. Charles I.)."

Arnold, in his history of Rhode Island, says of the Puritans: "In estimating their characters, we are too apt to judge them by the light of the present day. They founded a colony for their own faith, without any idea of tolerating others. For doing this, they have been charged with bigotry, fanaticism, and folly. Every epithet has been applied to them, that can be employed to express detestation of the conduct of men acting under a sober conviction of truth. Regarding their conduct from the standpoint of the nineteenth century, all this may be just. The like proceedings in this age, would deserve the severest sentence of condemnation. But not so, two hundred years ago. The bigotry of the Puritans was the bigotry of their times. In every act, they illustrated the spirit of the age." From this point of view, we must forgive them for the bitterness of a persecution which brought the life of Mary Dyre to an untimely end on the 1st of June, 1660. It has been said of her that she was "one of those rare spirits who are *predestined* to become martyrs and saints to the faith they profess." The sons of William and Mary Dyre were Samuel, William, Henry, Mahershalalhashbaz, and Charles. The following record shows that there were, at least, *two* daughters: "July 25, 1670, Samuel and Henry Dyre bind themselves to their father, William Dyre, to pay to their sister (eldest daughter of William) £100 within three years after the death of their father, and to Elizabeth Dyre (second daughter of William) the sum of £40 when eighteen years of age." The remarkable Scripture name given to the fourth son, can be found in the eighth chapter of Isaiah, first verse. It is a striking illustration of the great fondness for Old Testament names, which prevailed at that time,—a fondness which, it is said, brought Beelzebub into use. The tragic death of the wife and mother must have greatly saddened the lives of William Dyre and his family; but unfortunately, our accounts of them are very meagre. The commercial prosperity of Newport began early in the history of the country, when, owing to its magnificent harbor, it became one of the principal ports of the New World, and for a time rivalled New York in its general commerce, and surpassed it in the special branches of whaling and trade with Africa and the Indies. It is painful to add that many of the fortunes which were accumulated were the result of a vigorous prosecution of the African slave trade. On the breaking out of the

Revolutionary War, Newport was, to a great extent, deserted by its inhabitants and, being left in a defenceless state, was occupied by the British for the three years succeeding 1776. It was used for the most part as a naval station, though some 8000 English and Hessians were, during most of the time, either quartered in the town or encamped in its suburbs. When the town was evacuated in 1779, many buildings were wantonly destroyed. At this time, the inhabitants numbered only about 4000 souls; and although efforts were at once made to restore its prosperity as a commercial port, it never recovered from the depressing effects of British occupation. It is unfortunate that the *town records were either carried off, or destroyed by the British,* for, with them, was lost the only source of information regarding the glory of ante-Revolutionary Newport. The loss of these valuable documents prevents us from having much knowledge of the marriages, births, and deaths of members of the Dyre family, or their wills. Neither do we know what were their church relations. William Dyre, after the death of his wife, continued his public services, and was chosen Solicitor for the colony. In 1665, in a petition to the Commissioners, he offended the authorities by the freedom of his complaints; and "being reasoned with, admitted his fault, in writing, to the Assembly, and received pardon." On May 27th, 1669, it is recorded that "William Dyre, Secretary of the Councell, this day rendered up unto the Councell, the books and papers which belonged unto them, and also the seale." It is hardly possible that a life of such constant activity and care should pass without leaving its traces upon him, in various ways, and he must at times have been very weary of it. Many years had passed since he first landed in America, and how little peace, and quietness, he had known! His children, too, were beginning to leave him for other homes. William Dyre, Jr., about the time of his mother's death, went to the State of Delaware. There are many of his descendants, among the first families of Delaware and Maryland. The Wynkoops, Georges, Bradfords. the families of Judge Milligan, of Wilmington, and of the Hon. Lewis McLane, all belong to the Dyre genesis.

Samuel Dyre, the oldest son of William and Mary, married Ann Hutchinson, daughter of Captain Edward Hutchinson, and granddaughter of the famous Ann Hutchinson. She was also a grandniece of the poet, John Dryden. Mrs. Dyre's grandmother is described as "a woman of great intellectual endowments and of masculine energy, to whom even her enemies ascribed unusual mental powers, styling her "the masterpiece of woman's wit," and describing her as "a gentlewoman of an haughty carriage, busy spirit, competent wit, and a voluble tongue; who, by a remarkable union of charity, devotion and ability, soon became the leader not only of her own sex, but of a powerful party in the state and church, so that her opponents have termed her "The Nonsuch." She went first to Providence, and thence to Aquidneck, which had just been purchased by the fugitives of her party, and where her husband died in 1642. Soon after this bereavement, she removed with her family to a spot near Hurl Gate, within the Dutch jurisdiction, where, in a short time, she and, with the exception of one child, all her household, sixteen in number, were murdered by the Indians in 1643. Whether her granddaughter, Mrs. Samuel Dyre, inherited Mrs. Hutchinson's talents and graces, we do not know. Mrs. Dyre was early left a widow with two sons, Samuel and Edward, and September 22d, 1679, at Tower Hill, Narragansett, she married Daniel Vernon, a man of very superior education, who spoke several languages, and was long a tutor in the family of Lodowick Updike, in North Kingstown. She had three children after her marriage to Mr. Vernon—Daniel, Samuel, and Catharine; from them are sprung one of the most distinguished families of Newport. A descendant, William Vernon, was in familiar correspondence with La Fayette, Adams, Viscount Noailles, Franklin, and other men of note in his day. He was a great friend of learning, and was appointed president of the Redwood Library on the death of its founder and first president; and the Second Congregational Church owed much to his liberality. He entered heart and soul into the cause of freedom during the Revolution; and it is said that, " to his unflinching devotion to liberty, personal sacrifices, and extraordinary exertions, America, under Providence, owes much of her success upon the sea." Ann Dyre Vernon died January 10th, 1716, and her gravestone is still standing in the Vernon lot at Newport, beside that of her husband. Her father, Captain Edward Hutchinson, was actively engaged in King Philip's war, and commanded a body of troops. In his will, proved in Boston in 1675, he gives all his Narragansett lands to Elizabeth Winslow, Ann Dyre, and Susanna Hutchinson—the latter afterwards married Nathaniel Coddington.

The name of Samuel Dyre appears in various records. In 1661, land in Narragansett, called Misquamokuck (now Westerly), was taken by William Dyre, Sr., Samuel Dyre, and Mahershalalhashbaz Dyre, and articles of agreement between an Indian captain and others were signed by them. William Dyre was appointed to transcribe the deeds, testimonies, ratifications, etc. At a general meeting, February 17th, 1661-2, William Dyre was chosen surveyor of Misquamokuck. At the court held at Acquedneset, near Wickford, May 20th, 1671, the persons inhabiting here being called to give their engagement and desiring to know whether or no the court, on behalf of the colony, do lay any claim to their possessions which they now inhabit, which persons were Mr. Samuel Dyre and others. To which demand this present court do return unanimously this answer: That on behalf of the colony this court do not lay any claims to their possessions which they now inhabit. May 21st, 1669, Samuel Dyer, of Narragansett, was appointed one of two conservators of his Majesty's peace for the Narragansett country—the other being Richard Smith. The latter had, in 1639, established a trading post, and erected the first English dwelling at Wickford. In 1656, Mr. Smith leased of the Indians, for 66 years, all the land which now forms the present site of Wickford. A few years afterwards, he leased it again for a thousand years. In 1660, he received a quitclaim deed of nearly, if not quite all, of these lands. Some estimate may be formed of his extensive domain, when we find that the tract was nine miles long, and three miles in width. Roger Williams named the place Wickford, in honor of a lady guest of Richard Smith's. Smith bought also Mr. Williams' interest, including "his trading house, his two big guns, and a small island (Rabbit Island) for goats."

The following letter from Roger Williams, with reference to this estate of Richard Smith's, is so quaint that I cannot resist inserting it.

NAHIGGONSIK, 24th July, 1679, (ut vulgo).

"1st. I, Roger Williams, of Providence, in the Nahiggonsik bay in N. Engl., being (by God's mersie) ye first beginner of ye Towne of Providence and of ye Colony of Rhode Island and Providence Plantations, being now neere to Foure Score years of age, yet (by God's mersie) of sound understanding and memorie, doe humbly and faithfully declare yt Mr. Richard Smith, Senior, who, for his conscience to God, left faire possessions in Gloster Shire, and adventured with his Relations and Estate to N. Engl., and was a most acceptable Inhabitant and prime leading man in Taunton in Plymouth Colony. For his conscience' sake (many differences arising) he left Taunton, and came to ye

Nahiggonsik country, where, by God's mersie and ye fave of ye Nahiggonsik sachems he broke ye Ice (at his great Charge and Hazard) and put up in ye thickest of ye Barbarians ye first English House amongst them.

"2d. I humbly testifieyt about forty years (from this date) he kept Possession, comming and going himselfe, children and servants, and he had quiet Possession of his Howsing, Lands and meadow, and there, in his own house, with much serenity of soule and comfort, he yielded up his spirit to God, ye Father of Spirits, in Peace."

Never a claim to land in New England was involved in greater uncertainty than this. The fight for its possession lasted long after Roger Williams had been placed in his grave. All the surrounding colonies became gradually involved in it. Rhode Island came near being entirely absorbed by Massachusetts and Connecticut. Many were the traditions of long-continued wars and bloody conflicts; and his Indian neighbors had to tell when Richard Smith settled in Wickford, in the year of our Lord 1639.

In October 1674, just before King Philip's war, and a generation after Richard Smith had taken up his abode within it borders, Kings Towne was incorporated. It thus became the seventh town in the colony of Rhode Island, although, in point of fact, it was probably the third settlement. In 1679, the incorporation was reaffirmed. In 1722 the town was divided into North and South Kingstown, the act of legislature providing that North Kingstown be considered the elder town. These towns were generally known as the "Narragansett country," and their history is full of interest and romance. In South Kingstown occurred the great Narragansett Swamp Fight between the English and the Indians, which resulted in the destruction of the Narragansetts as a tribe. Commodore Oliver Hazard Perry, the hero of Lake Erie, was born in South Kingstown.

The town of East Greenwich was founded in May, 1677. Five thousand acres were granted to fifty persons in consideration of services rendered in King Philip's war, who thus became proprietors of the town, and founders of the new settlement of East Greenwich. The early settlers expected great things of the town. The liberality with which they laid out the streets, shows that they meant that it should be worthy of its future greatness. The names which they bestowed upon them, King, Queen, Marlboro', Duke, London, etc., are proofs of their loyalty to the mother country. In the year 1709, the town purchased a tract of land adjoining its western border, containing thirty-five thousand acres. The first Collector was Thomas Arnold. East Greenwich has the honor to have printed the first calico in America; some time previous to 1794, a man named Dawson erected print works. Jemima Wilkinson had a meeting-house there about 1774. On the 31st of October, 1677, one hundred acres of the five thousand were allotted to Henry Dyre. He had also, in 1670 and in 1680, received land by deed from his father, William Dyre, and his brother Samuel. Whether Henry Dyre resided on his land in East Greenwich I have no means of knowing. He died in February, 1690, aged 43 years. When I was in that pretty town in September, 1883, I found but few old records in the office of the town clerk, and most unfortunately, the town records of North Kingstown were destroyed by fire, some years ago. Undoubtedly in the probate proceedings, much valuable information might have been obtained, which is now forever lost. It is well known, however, that members of the Dyre family settled on lands bordering on Narragansett Bay. Beautiful estates they were, and tradition tells us of the style which was long kept up among them. In the days of slavery, the colored coachman and footman in livery, were by no means uncommon, and the land was tilled and cultivated by slave labor. When slavery was done away with, they probably took the plough in their own hands, and could heartily sing with Burns, "A man's a man for a' that." At what time the name was changed from *Dyre* to *Dyer* is not known. In a family cemetery of North Kingston I found one stone only with the old spelling: that of Captain Samuel *Dyre*, who died April 4th, 1791, in the 34th year of his age. Probably the new spelling was adopted by degrees. The name certainly was not *improved* by the change, and it is a pity that the spelling of years, was not retained.

In a book recently published in England, I find

further notices of *William Dyre*. It is entitled, "Dorothea Scott, of Egerton House, Kent, 1611 to 1680, by G. D. Scull, editor of 'The Evelyns in America.' Printed for private circulation by Perker & Co., Oxford, 1883." It is stated in the book that one John Scott, who came to America, had defrauded Mrs. Dorothea Scott, who "did intrust him with the whole concernes of her estate, which in the end proved fatal to her." The Duke of York commanded Samuel Pepys, Secretary to the Admiralty, to collect evidence against Scott. This Samuel Pepys is the author of the "Diary" much read and quoted. He had an interview with Captain William Dyre in London, on the 19th September, 1679, and engaged him to collect information in New York and elsewhere, concerning Scott's antecedents in America. Captain Dyre wrote to Pepys "from on board ye ship *Bever*, in ye Downes, ye 2^d of 8ber., 1679." and incidentally mentioned that Mr. Randolph "sends his service." This was Edward Randolph, Charles II.'s commissioner to New England, who made eight voyages across the Atlantic in nine years. Thomas Lovelace, an important witness for Pepys, was making a visit to England in 1680, and on his return that year to New York, Pepys gave him letters of introduction to Captain Dyre and Sir Edmund Andross. (This Captain Dyre, it is stated, was the husband of Mary Dyre, who was executed in 1660, in Boston, for her professions of Quakerism. It is also stated that the descendants of William Dyre spelled their name Dyer.) Samuel Pepys writes to William Dyre :

"September 20th, 1679.

"SIR: Were it not yt ye Honour of his Majesties and his service is more concerned in it than any interest of my owne, I should not hold it so excusable in me to offer ye trouble I am now designing you; but knowing how acceptable anything is to you wherein His Honour and ye Justice due to His Ministers is concerned, I take ye liberty of putting into your hands an Extract of a letter relating to severall partics by him therein charged upon one Captain John Scott. I am to desire y^t so soon as you shall be received where you are now going (and towards wch I wish you a happy voyage), you will use ye speediest and most effectuall means you can of informing yourselfe, and enabling me to report to his Majesty, what evidences you can collect of ye truth of ye particulars menc'oned in ye said Extract, and of whatever undue behaviours you shall (upon inquiry into ye legend of Scott's life in New England, Long Island, and parts adjacent) obtaine ye certaine knowledge of. W^{ch} takeing ye liberty of recommending to you, I beg you to favour me wth any commands of yours wherein I may, in some measure, answer yor respect to me in this particular, assuring you of my being, with all faithfulness, y^r most humble servant, SAMUEL PEPYS."

The following letter was written to Samuel Pepys by William Dyre, dated:

NEW YORK^e, 4th January, 1680.

"WORTHY SIR: Yours of the 24th Aug^t, by Mr.

Lovelace, I have received, for which great favour of correspondence I own myselfe much obliged, and am unexpressibly rejoiced that Sir Anthony and yourselfe are out of ye pernitious power of that villain Scott, whome, doubtlesse, the hands of Justice one day will reach for all his horrid contrivances and practices wth condign punishment. You may please to know hee has a son now gone from here to England, to seek out his ffather, hearing that hee was famous in ye kingdome. But I doubt ye young man will be disappointed in his expedition; hee can certainly informe you that his mother is alive in ye province, and yett, as wee heare, old Scott had the Impudence to make his addresses to ye Lady Vane, and that in a very splendid manner, and had not Death (which some say hee occasioned) put a period to her days, he had most miserably deluded, deceived, and abused her ladyship. Sir, you will (by the occasion of some like Coll. Scott), have the advantage of seeing my Governor, Sir Edmund Andross, in England, who, doubtless, is a person of that great worth and honour as not to have his name or reputation blemished by anything but what is false, envious, and malicious, which has caused the Dukes desires of seeing him at home with all speed, and soe hath given his Excellency the trouble and danger of a severe winter's voyage; but I hope ye sunshine of his happy returne to us in the Spring, will dispell all those malevolent clouds, and render the people of theis country (under his Maj^ties and Royal Highness dominion) as fortunate as formerly by his prudence and noble government, the continuance of which, together with your health and prosperity, is the hearty desire of yours, etc. etc., WILLIAM DYRE."

England was at this time having serious difficulty with the Dutch, and it may have been that loyalty to his native land, took William Dyre to England. It has been hinted that he "did a little privateering on his own account, and that privateering *then*, was common with respectable persons." This charge has never been sustained, and the esteem in which he was held seems to contradict any accusation of unfair or dishonest dealing. In a letter from Roger Williams to his "dear and loving friends and neighbors, of Providence and Warwick," dated from the residence of Sir Henry Vane, at Belleau, in Lincolnshire, April 1st, 1653, he says: "I hope it may have pleased the Most High Lord of sea and land, to bring *dear Mr. Dyre* unto you." After 1680 we lose all trace of William Dyre. In that year he was collector of customs at New York for the Duke of York. Undoubtedly the town records taken so unceremoniously, by the British, from Newport would have told the tale, now lost to us forever. It is probable that advanced age kept him in America for the rest of his days, and that he died on his Newport farm in 1681. His friend, Roger Williams, died in 1683, aged 84, and it is known that the death of William Dyre occurred before that time. As they had been so closely and intimately connected in life, it is pleasant to know that their descendants have kept up the friendly tie, there having been several intermarriages among them. Some of our best and most valued citizens are proud to claim descent from these alliances.

It has been impossible to trace the history of *all* the children of William and Mary Dyre; but I have been able to find the most important facts with reference to the descent of the branch of the family in which I am most interested, and it is this:

First. William and Mary Dyre.

Second. Samuel, their eldest son, baptized in Boston, December 20th, 1635. Married Anne Hutchinson, daughter of Captain Edward Hutchinson, granddaughter of the celebrated Anne Hutchinson, great granddaughter of the Rev. Edward Marbury, of Lincolnshire, England, and grandniece of the poet John Dryden.

May 21st, 1669, Samuel Dyre was appointed one of two conservators of his Majesty's peace for the Narragansett country, and was long engaged in promoting the settlement of that country.

Third. Edward Dyre, son of Samuel and Anne Hutchinson Dyre, was born in 1670. He married Mary ———. Owned a farm in North Kingstown. May 7th, 1712, he petitions to the General Assembly of Rhode Island concerning a highway near his land.

Fourth. Edward Dyre, Jr., son of Edward and Mary was born in North Kingstown, January 6th, 1701—lived in North Kingstown, and was made freeman, May 1st, 1722. In 1748 was deputy to the General Assembly from North Kingstown.

Fifth. Edward Dyre (son of Edward, Jr.) was born in North Kingstown in 1725. Was made freeman in May, 1752. Married Elizabeth Fish, Nov. 29th, 1750. Their children were William, Charles, Frances, Benjamin, Amherst, *Henry,* Susannah, Anna, Elizabeth.

Sixth. Henry Dyre (son of Edward Dyre, 3d) was born in North Kingstown, July 12th, 1759. On the 19th of March, 1787, he married Sarah Coy. Soon after his marriage he went to Shaftesbury, Vermont, and there the following children were born: Moses, Anna, Olive, Lydia, Rufus, Dennis, David, Daniel, Lewis, Heman. His son Dr. Lewis Dyer speaks thus of him: "My father was a modest man. He was a great reader, especially of history. When he went to school he walked three miles, twice a day. He cultivated intellectual arithmetic with much interest, and in his old age, when his sons were at home, would often reach results by mental process in half the time it required them by the use of slate and pencil. There was much of the 'old school gentleman' about him."

Henry Dyer died January 2d, 1855, aged 95 years. Sarah Coy Dyer died July 26th, 1846, aged 77. Their last years were spent on a farm delightfully situated in the valley between the Green and Equinox ranges of mountains, near the beautiful village of Manchester, Vermont. In this secluded home they reared their family of children, giving them every educational advantage possible, and fitting them for useful citizens. No iron road then ran through that remote valley, no shrill whistle echoing through the mountains gave to those dwellers in rural homes intimations of the stir, the gatherings, the quick life, the accelerated movements of the populations of cities. They were far away from great centres, which did not, as they now do, report themselves daily—transmit daguerreotypes of their busy, bustling scenes to the quiet village and the lonely farm-house. Children reared amid such surroundings must often have longed to pass those mountain barriers, and as the family of Henry Dyer on "Equinox Farm" grew up, they left their home on the hillside, to take their part in the battle of life. The farm, however, still remains in the family, and is now owned by Douglas Henry Dyer, a grandson of Henry Dyer, Senior. The two following sketches are of the youngest sons of Henry and Sarah Coy Dyer.

Lewis Dyer, M.D., son of Henry and Sarah Coy Dyer, was born in Shaftesbury, Vermont, February 24th, 1807. He graduated December, 1828, at the Berkshire Medical Institute, Massachusetts, which was organized under the charter of Williams College. After practicing a few years, at Gloversville, New York, he emigrated westward in the summer of 1832. While visiting his brother, Rev. Heman Dyer, D.D., then connected with Kenyon College, Gambier, Ohio, the trustees of the college and theological seminary, offered him the position of physician to these institutions, which he accepted, and filled for a few years. That field being too limited for professional labor, he moved to Mount Vernon, in the same county, where he shared, for a time, an office with the Hon. Columbus Delano, late Secretary of the Interior—the one dispensing physic—the other, law and metaphysics. While here he edited the Whig newspaper of the city, and was a member of the Ohio Whig State Convention, called to consider what action should be taken consequent upon the repeal of the Missouri Compromise. While some advocated its restoration, Dr. Dyer said, "Let it stand repealed, but never admit another slave State into the Union." In 1855 he moved to Iowa, but the winters were too severe for his wife and daughter, and, declining a professorship in a medical college at Keokuk, he sought a more genial climate at Du Quoin, Illinois. When the late war broke out he was instrumental in sending many soldiers into the field and, at the personal request of Governor Yates, accepted the position of surgeon to the Eighty-first Illinois regiment, to which office this regiment elected him. On the day he entered the field he was placed upon the operating staff, where he remained for two years, after which he was promoted to the office of surgeon-in-chief of division, the duties of which were both grave and arduous. In justice to the subject of this notice, an episode in his army life should here be noted. Two or three officers of the line, having become displeased with the Doctor, succeeded, by subornation of perjury, in having certain charges secretly preferred against him and forwarded to the Secretary of War. It was a month, or more, before this conspiracy came to the Doctor's knowledge. It was then communicated by his colonel, who advised him to resign. This he indignantly refused to do; as, under the circumstances, it would be an admission of guilt and both dishonorable and cowardly.

He now repaired to General Grant's headquarters and, on learning that a document containing certain charges had been received and forwarded to the Secretary of War, inquired what an innocent, honorable and determined man should do, to vindicate himself. Whereupon General Grant at once issued an order to General McPherson to convene a court of inquiry, forthwith, to investigate the matter. Such a court was convened, and the evidence elicited by it not only exculpated the Doctor, but brought to light one of the foulest conspiracies on record. The proceedings of the court, with a letter from General McPherson, were forwarded to the War Department; but, meantime, an order dismissing Dr. Dyer from the service, with the loss of all pay, was received and read at dress parade. The Doctor was present, and remarked: "Gentlemen, this matter will not end here!" Doffing his shoulder straps, and repairing to General McPherson's headquarters, he said to that officer: "General, I have come to tender my services to carry a musket in the ranks!" The corps medical director, who was present, interposed by saying. "If Dr. Dyer wishes to volunteer, I shall be very glad to assign him to duty, as we need his services very much." This arrangement was entered upon, but shortly terminated by the prompt restoration of the Doctor to his former position. He was regarded by his associates as a skillful, brave and noble officer. A high compliment was paid him, when, at the close of the war, the history of the Illinois troops being called for, by an act of the Legislature, Dr. Dyer was assigned to the duty of writing the history of his command. It must be a pleasant reflection that, being himself the son of a Revolutionary soldier, who fought to *establish* our government and institutions, he and his two sons, during "the great rebellion," fought to *save* them. Returning to Du Quoin after the war, he resumed his profession, and has pursued it ever since, conscious of the confidence and good will of the public and profession, generally. He has ever been an active and efficient member and once the president of the Southern Illinois Medical Association—a body of two hundred physicians, all graduates. In 1875, the office of United States examining surgeon was offered him, which he accepted. During the last year, the board, of which he is president, examined over five hundred pensioners. He is the friend of popular education, and much of his life has been connected with educational interests. In politics he is a Republican, but believes the party has been needlessly demoralized by the unscrupulous conduct of demagogues. He has delivered numerous public addresses and lectures on a variety of subjects. On General Grant's return to the United States, after his voyage around the world, and his visit to Mexico, Dr. Dyer, by appointment of his fellow citizens, delivered to him the address of welcome, on his arrival at Du Quoin. He commenced as follows:

"GENERAL GRANT: I need not say, this assemblage of people has no political significance whatever. We are met to greet you, and to welcome you home to your native land.

"We have met to show respect to the distinguished general and the magnanimous conqueror; the ex-President of the United States, the renowned traveller,—and the illustrious citizen. We have met to show respect to the private citizen who has been honored above all other men, living or dead, by the crowned heads of Europe and Asia; and who, in the presence of royalty and amid the blandishments of court etiquette and the dazzling splendor of oriental nations, has never uttered a sentiment compromising his personal dignity and his exalted personal character; but who has always proved the faithful and true exponent of the principles and institutions of his own glorious country."

Dr. Dyer has had a large experience in presiding over conventions and public assemblies. He was president of the large Republican club of the city in which he lives, during the campaigns of Grant, Hayes and Garfield. The most notable occasion of this kind was at a Congressional convention held at Cairo, Illinois, a year or two ago, to nominate a candidate for Congress, which, during its two days' and two nights' continuance, threatened, several times, to break up in a row, and would have done so but for Dr. Dyer's level head and firm hand. His life has always been a useful and active one. In December, 1883, he writes to a friend, " I shall be, according to tradition, seventy-seven years old next February, and this has been one of the busiest years of my life!"

The Rev. Heman Dyer, D. D., was born in the town of Shaftesbury, Bennington county, Vermont, on the 10th of September, 1810. He was the son of Henry and Sarah Coy Dyer. His father and all his uncles on his father's side served in the war of the Revolution. One of his uncles became a captain in the service.

While Dr. Dyer was yet a child, about six years of age, his father removed to Manchester in the same county and State. Here he spent the rest of his childhood and early youth, attending the district school during the winter and working on the farm in the summer. When in his fifteenth year he created quite a sensation by commencing the study of Latin, a thing unheard of at that day in a district school. In his sixteenth or seventeenth year he was sent to the academy in Arlington in the same county. Here he pursued his studies preparatory to entering college. Among his instructors were the Rev. Anson B. Hard, the principal of the academy, and the Rev. Dr. Coit, the rector of the parish. To these instructors he became strongly attached, and for them he ever after cherished the sincerest respect.

During this period Dr. Dyer taught the district

school in two of the neighborhoods in Arlington, spending in all about eight months in this occupation. As he was much younger than many of his scholars, he had to assume an air of dignity and importance, which seemed rather comical to himself and his friends. It being the custom for the school-master and the school-mistress to board round among all the families of the district, he thus acquired a kind of knowledge and experience, which served a most valuable purpose during the rest of his life. While pursuing his studies in Arlington, there occurred an incident which shaped, very largely, his whole future career. It had been his wish and ambition to enter and go through either Middlebury College or the University at Burlington, both in his native State, but one day at the academy there was put in his hand, by some one, a leaflet entitled "The Star in the West," after the fashion of Dr. Buchanan's "Star in the East." This leaflet was prepared and sent out by the Rt. Rev. Philander Chase, D. D., the first bishop of Ohio, and was a plea and appeal in behalf of education and Christian missions in the West. Bishop Chase was then engaged in founding Kenyon College, and the other institutions at Gambier. The appeal so stirred up the young student that he resolved at once to go to Ohio, at the earliest day practicable. When he made his resolution known to his classmates and others, they were amazed; admiring, no doubt, his pluck more than his wisdom. They could not understand how a young a man should be willing to go so far from home, and busy himself in such a wilderness as Ohio then was. Fortunately his parents did not oppose the idea, but rather encouraged it.

Accordingly, at the close of his second engagement as a teacher, about the 20th of April, 1829, he left his home, and the East, for the West. The West was then most emphatically in Ohio. He made the journey from Manchester to Gambier—about the centre of the State—entirely by stage, consuming fourteen days and nights in continuous traveling. He reached Gambier early in May, a perfect stranger, and without even a note of introduction from anybody to anybody. He commenced his studies without delay, hoping to enter the Freshman class in Kenyon College at the beginning of the next term, which he succeeded in doing. As student, teacher, tutor, and head of one of the departments of the institution, he remained in Gambier ten years and a half. For two years and more, he occupied the anomalous position of a student and also of a member of the faculty. While in these double relations, he became acquainted with, and rendered some valuable services to, Edwin M. Stanton, afterward the great War Secretary in President Lincoln's cabinet; Mr. Stanton never forgot these services. During these ten and a half years, Dr. Dyer took his degrees of A. B. and A. M. While yet a student he was elected as secretary of the Diocesan Convention, and treasurer of the Episcopal fund. It was during this period that the difficulties arose between Bishop Chase and the faculty, with regard to the administration of the institutions. These difficulties were followed by the resignation of the Bishop both as president of the college, and Bishop of the diocese. Subsequently, upon the election of Dr. McIlvaine to succeed Bishop Chase, Dr. Dyer was sent East to lay before the Bishop-elect the official documents connected with the election and such other information as might be desired. After Bishop McIlvaine took charge of the diocese, Dr. Dyer was ordained by him, both as deacon and as presbyter. In his many and varied duties he was constantly occupied until the spring of 1840, when he removed to Pittsburgh, Penn., and established a classical school there. At the head of this school he continued for three years or more, when he was elected to a professorship in the Western University of Pennsylvania. After serving for one year as professor he was elected principal or, as it was subsequently called, chancellor of the institution. About this time he received the degree of D.D. from Trinity College, Hartford. He was then in the 34th year of his age. In the great fire in Pittsburgh the University Buildings, with the library and apparatus, were entirely destroyed. Within a year new buildings were erected and the institution was prosperous, but the health of Dr. Dyer was very much shattered by his many cares and labors, and in 1849 he resigned his connection with the University and removed to Philadelphia, where he had been invited to perform certain duties in connection with the American Sunday School Union. He continued in this connection from February, 1849, to January, 1854. In

1852 he and his wife visited Europe, spending between six and seven months.

About a year after his return from Europe, he was elected Corresponding Secretary and General Manager of the Protestant Episcopal Society for the Promotion of Evangelical Knowledge, commonly called the Evangelical Knowledge Society. This society was formed in 1847, and had for one of its objects the meeting and counteracting of certain tendencies in the Episcopal Church, which had been largely awakened and promoted by the somewhat famous Oxford, or Tractarian, movement in England.

He accepted the new position to which he had been appointed, and removed to New York early in 1854. The duties to which he was now called brought him more or less into antagonism with many of the leading influences of his church. He met the charge of disloyalty brought against the new society, by inducing the Executive Committee to bring out the Book of Common Prayer in three or four different sizes, and give it the widest possible circulation. For several years this society distributed more prayer books than all the other societies put together. This action was a practical and logical answer to the criticisms which had been made.

From 1854 to 1861, he was constantly employed in his duties at the office of the society in New York, and in visiting various parts of the country, to attend diocesan conventions and public meetings, and to preach and make addresses in the interest of the society.

In 1861, when the war broke out, the society was actively engaged in publishing books, tracts, and two periodicals, the *Parish Visitor* and the *Standard Bearer*. Up to this time the duties of editor-in-chief had been discharged, first, by the Rev. John S. Stone, D. D., and afterwards by the Rev. C. W. Andrews, D. D., of Virginia. As the war interrupted all regular intercouse with the South, Dr. Dyer was requested to act as editor of the society's publications and periodicals; this added very largely to his cares and responsibilities. In 1861 the American Church Missionary Society was organized, and Dr. Dyer was appointed Corresponding Secretary. About the same time the New York branch of the Christian Commission was established, and he became its local secretary, the Hon. Nathan Bishop being the chief secretary. He was also made a director of the American Bible Society. In 1862 he was elected the first Bishop of the new Diocese of Kansas, which office he declined to accept. During the war he was appointed on several occasions to visit Washington, with others, in behalf of the work of the Christian Commission. On one occasion he was taken by Secretary Stanton into a cabinet meeting and, on introducing him to Mr. Lincoln, the Secretary said, "Mr. President, I wish to introduce to you my old friend, the Rev. Dr. Dyer, of New York; he was my friend when I *needed* a friend." To which the President, stretching out his long arm and grasping the Doctor's hand, and shaking it vigorously, responded: "I am glad to see you, sir; I am glad to know any one who helped to make my Secretary of War, for I don't know what *I* should have done without him." With that, Mr. Seward, Mr. Fessenden, and others of the cabinet clapped their hands, and cried " Good, good."

During one of his visits to Washington he went, in company with the Rev. Dr. Butler, to see the magnificent army of General McClellan of some 200,000 men, encamped a few miles from Washington. Dr. Dyer's only son was at this time a soldier in this army. While dining with the captain of the company to which his son belonged, they were startled by the sudden order for the regiments to form and prepare for battle. At once the whole scene was changed, and infantry, cavalry and artillery were in motion; the dinner and all ceremony were cut short, and the two Doctors of Divinity hastened to their horse and wagon, which an orderly had charge of, and commenced a rapid advance in a direction quite opposite to that towards which the troops were moving.

The battle proved to be the short and sharp skirmish of Drainesville. But it enabled the visitors to see the great army in motion, and marching in columns, six or eight deep, and at double quick time. On another occasion, when Dr. Dyer was called to Washington to see his son who was confined in one of the hospitals there, Mr. Stanton showed him much attention by having him spend the whole morning with him in his office at the War Department, and the afternoon with him and his family at their private residence. Before leaving, the Secretary surprised the Doctor by giving him, to take to his son, at the hospital, a captain's commission, and the copy of an order appointing him to duty, as soon as he should be able to leave, in the commissary department in New York. He also offered the Doctor an appointment to an important position in connection with the chaplain service, which he felt bound to decline. These friendly relations between the two parties continued till the death of Mr. Stanton.

During the war Dr. Dyer took an active part with Bishop Alonzo Potter and others, in establishing and endowing the Philadelphia Divinity School. For many years he was a member of its Board of Management. At the close of the war, and at the request of several prominent laymen of New York, he visited the Theological Seminary of Virginia, and some of the government officials at Washington, in reference to the restoration of the buildings and grounds of the institution, so that they might again be used for their original purposes. For a considerable time they had been occupied as hospitals, and needed many repairs. At a later period he visited Richmond in Virginia and Charleston, South Carolina, to ascertain the condition of things in the South and the best methods of extending needed aid on the part of Northern friends. These visits resulted in much pecuniary assistance to individuals and institutions in that part of the country.

Dr. Dyer took an active part in the formation of the "Latimer Society," and afterwards of the "Clerical

Association,"—both located in New York, and established in the interests of evangelical religion. In these and many other associations, he was incessantly occupied, and to a degree that most seriously impaired his health.

In 1868 it became evident that he must have rest, or completely break down. Accordingly, it was so arranged that he could be relieved of his duties; and early in the spring, accompanied by his wife and daughter, he sailed for Europe, where he spent several months in England and Scotland and on the Continent. On his return in October, a breakfast was given him by his friends, in one of the public halls. In the autumn of 1869 Dr. Dyer met with a most serious railroad accident. He was on his way from Troy to Manchester, Vt. Heavy rains had produced very high water in all the streams, and much damage had been done to the railroads. Consequently, the trains were running very irregularly. Just before the train on which he had taken passage reached Lansingburg, at a sharp turn of the road, it came into collision with a train coming from the north. The crash was terrible, and the cars of both trains were piled on top of one another in a most indescribable manner. Only one person was killed, but many were injured. This occasioned a delay for several hours. It was raining very heavily. Night came on, and everything was shrouded in darkness and gloom. The conductor told the few passengers in the car that he would take them to Hoosick Falls, where they would find hotel accommodations. On reaching the Hoosick River, it was found to be very much swollen, and the passengers were requested to leave the cars and cross the bridge on foot, as it was not safe to attempt to take the locomotive and cars across it. With much difficulty the bridge was crossed, and at about 9 o'clock in the evening some ten or fourteen passengers got on the locomotive and tender, which were found on the other side of the river. Dr. Dyer was on the locomotive, near the engineer. After going about three-fourths of a mile they came to a curve in the road, where the river, now swollen to a raging flood, had, during the preceding hour, completely swept out the foundation of the road, but the rails appeared to be undisturbed. As soon as the locomotive came upon this spot, both it and the tender went down, instantly, into the fearful chasm, a distance of some thirty or forty feet. Most of those on the tender jumped off, and thus saved themselves. All on the locomotive were carried down into the raging waters. Several were killed instantly. Dr. Dyer was carried down with the others; but, extricating himself from the locomotive, he was swept away by the current, and being a good swimmer, he succeeded at last in making a landing about three quarters of a mile down the river and was saved, though he was terribly bruised. He never recovered his usual health and strength after this accident. The shock to his nervous system was too great to pass permanently away.

As early as 1865 Dr. Dyer was appointed a member

of the Foreign Committee of the Board of Missions, which added very much to his labors. When the Board established commissions for work among the freedmen of the South and the Indians in our Western States and Territories, he was placed upon the executive committees of each of these bodies, and made chairman of that for the Indian Commission. This made it necessary for him to carry on an extensive correspondence, and to have frequent personal intercourse with the Secretary of the Interior, the Commissioner of Indian Affairs, and other officials at Washington. As the nomination of Indian agents for all the reservations assigned by the government to the Episcopal Church devolved upon his committee, Dr. Dyer became painfully acquainted with the plans and schemes and wicked devices of politicians, great and small, in carrying out and accomplishing their personal and selfish ends in this branch of the public service. He often spoke of the conduct of men holding the highest political, and even moral, trusts with the severest disapprobation and disgust; and very glad was he when, by a change in the policy of the government, as well as of the church, he was relieved of this most unpleasant service.

In 1873 a meeting of the Evangelical Alliance took place in New York. As a member of one of the committees, Dr. Dyer took a deep and active interest in the proceedings of this body. In the same year, what has been termed the "Cummins Movement," that is, the secession of one Bishop and several of the clergy from the Episcopal Church, took place. While Dr. Dyer sympathized with some of the difficulties under which these brethren labored, he did not think that secession was the best way of curing the evils complained of. The whole country had had a notable illustration of the difficulties and dangers of secession, and he did not think such an experiment should be tried in the church. He took strong ground in favor of fighting the battle out within the church, feeling very sure that in the end all needed relief would be obtained, and that thus, even the appearance of schism would be avoided.

About the same time the movement in England, and in this country, took place with regard to Bible revision. Dr. Dyer took a lively interest in this undertaking, and served on the American Finance Committee for many years. In 1875 he was appointed to accompany Bishop Lee, of Delaware, in his visit to Mexico to inquire into the present condition and future promise of the evangelistic work there going on under the administration of the Rev. Henry C. Riley, D.D. In this expedition he was accompanied by his wife and daughter, and other friends. About two months were thus occupied.

At the General Convention of 1877, the old Board of Missions, consisting of several hundred members, was abolished, and in its place a Board of Managers, consisting, exclusive of the Bishops, of fifteen clergymen and fifteen laymen, was created. To this Board the conduct of our general church missionary work, at home, and in foreign countries, was committed. Dr. Dyer was appointed by the Convention a member of this Board, and was assigned for duty in the Foreign department.

In 1879 he was elected by the Convention of the Diocese of New York as a trustee of the General Theological Seminary. This was a great surprise to him, and many of his friends. So pronounced had been his views, particularly as to the former administration of the institution, that it seemed incredible the Convention of New York should elect him to such a post. Some of his friends criticised rather severely his acceptance of this position. But his reply was that, having had no knowledge of, or anything to do with the election, he felt it was his duty to avail himself of the opportunity of doing what he could to make the Seminary what it should be—general in the spirit of its administration, as well as in its name. Soon after his election he was made a member of the Standing Committee, and was appointed on two special committees having charge of a revision of the statutes, as well as the constitution of the institution. To the work of these committees he gave much attention, and had the satisfaction of seeing their recommendations adopted first by the Standing Committee, then by the Board of Trustees, and finally by the General Convention in 1883. The character of some of the changes made will be understood from the fact that the old Board consisted of several hundred members, and from all the dioceses, and was a constantly increasing body, as the church grew. The new Board, exclusive of the bishops, consists of fifty members, of which twenty-five are to be appointed by certain dioceses to represent certain pecuniary endowments, and twenty-five are to be appointed triennially by the General Convention. Of this latter number Dr. Dyer was appointed a member by the General Convention of 1883, his name standing first on the list.

His only motive in accepting this trust, as well as some others which had been committed to him, was to recognize the great change which had taken place in the general spirit and tone of the different parties in the church, and to give expression to that catholicity for which he had labored so long and so earnestly. While his views of church polity remained substantially the same as they had been throughout his life, he thought it the part of wisdom and of a true liberality, to adapt the *policy* of the church to the altered state of sentiment and feeling which so generally prevailed. Some there were who considered his course somewhat inconsistent, but he regarded it as entirely consistent with the principles he had always advocated, and as the only honest and honorable course to pursue.

During Dr. Dyer's life in New York he performed a large amount of clerical and other duty, outside of the societies with which he was more especially connected. Soon after his removal to the city he was asked to take charge of the Church of the Incarnation, which for a time had been a chapel of Grace Church. The rector of the new parish, Dr. Harwood, was obliged to leave his charge, and the city, on account of illness. Dr. Dyer supplied the pulpit for several months, including the Lenten and Easter season. During this time, he prepared and presented to the Bishop quite a large class for confirmation. Immediately upon the close of his services at the Incarnation, he was elected an assistant minister by the vestry of St. George's Church. In this relation he continued for five years. While the rector, the Rev. Dr. Tyng, was absent in Europe, he occupied the pulpit for six months, and performed more or less parochial duty. On several different occasions he had charge of the pulpits at St. Mark's, the Ascension, the Nativity, Calvary, Mediator, the Anthon Memorial; and also of St. Ann's and Christ Church, Brooklyn; Trinity Church, Newark; and Trinity, of Bergen Point, N. J. In this last-named parish he performed many services during the period of its organization, and on many occasions afterwards. At many different times he was put in charge of Christ Church, Bay Ridge. During the absence of the rector, the Rev. Mr. Aspinwall, in Europe, he, with his family, occupied the rectory, and he had entire charge of the parish, for more than a year. In all of the aforenamed churches he rendered services for from three to nine months each. For more than a year he held morning and afternoon services, and established a Sunday-school in the chapel of the Rutgers Institute on Fifth Avenue, near Forty-second street.

It was during the period of these services, that he

organized the Church of the Holy Trinity. On the evenings of the Sundays, he officiated at the chapel of the Rutgers Institute, he preached regularly in a hall in West Forty-second street, at a mission started by the Church of the Ascension. Among the laborers at the time in the mission, were Bishop Whittaker, of Nevada, and his wife. This mission grew into what became known as the "Memorial Chapel," with its chapel building and its settled pastors. He also performed many services at another mission of the Church of the Ascension, afterwards called the Chapel of the Comforter. He had charge, at different times, of the services at the Church of the Mediator, the building for which, on Lexington Avenue, was purchased by his friends, Mr. Wolfe and Mrs. Spencer.

Dr. Dyer rendered occasional services in many other churches, chapels, and missions. As a rule, he officiated from two to three times on Sundays, and very frequently during the week.

Dr. Dyer was an active friend and worker in behalf of St. Luke's Hospital from its commencement. He was for many years on its Board of Management, and was elected the president of the corporation, but declined to accept the office, thinking it ought to be held by a layman. He was also much interested in, and coöperated with his revered friend, Dr. Muhlenberg, in establishing St. Johnland. He gave much time and labor, in organizing "The Home for Incurables." For these three last-named institutions he was instrumental in raising a large amount of funds.

In 1872 or '73 he became a member of the Clerical Club, of which the Rev. Dr. E. A. Washburn was the chief originator. One of the outgrowths of the club was the Church Congress. Dr. Dyer was active in promoting the interests of both of these associations. For a long time he acted as chairman of the club, and presided at the breakfast given to Dean Stanley, during his visit to this country. He was for a long period the chairman of the Executive Committee of the Congress, and its meetings were held at his office in the Bible House. The interest he had in these associations arose largely from the conviction he had that their influence would be in the line of a broader and deeper and, consequently, truer catholicity throughout our church.

During Dr. Dyer's life in New York he was instrumental in raising large amounts of money for specific objects—objects outside of missionary and other causes, for which collections are taken in churches, or by any other systematic methods. From the books of record which he was in the habit of keeping, it would appear that more than $500,000 were received, and disbursed by him, for charitable purposes. The kind of reputation which he thus acquired, gave him not a little labor and trouble, and sometimes annoyance.

It will be seen, from the foregoing, that Dr. Dyer has led an exceedingly busy and laborious life, and that he has been associated with many leading characters, and connected with many societies, both local and general.

Several of the East Greenwich and North Kingstown branches of the Dyer family left Rhode Island and went to Vermont. The fame of that beautiful mountain region had spread all over New England, in the latter part of the last, and early part of the present century, causing a large emigration from the different States.

The following sketches are of other descendants of William and Mary Dyre:

CHARLES VOLNEY DYER.

A Sketch of His Long and Useful Career, Which is Closely Interwoven with the Early History of Chicago.

ONE more of the historic men who helped to make Chicago, passed away April 24, 1878, in the death of the venerable Dr. Charles Volney Dyer, one of the oldest and best known pioneers of the city, who died of paralysis at the residence of his son-in-law, *Mr. Adolph Heile* (Mr. Heile married a daughter *by adoption*), in the town of Lake View. He was born at Clarendon, Vt., on the 12th of June, 1808, and was, therefore, rounding up the full measure of his three score and ten, at his demise. His father, Daniel Dyer, was one of those sturdy old Green Mountain men, who did right gallant service in the days of the Revolution. His mother was Susan, daughter of Gideon and sister of Judge Abraham Olin, a woman of some note in her time, and whose character may be judged from the fact that she rode on horseback, unattended, a distance of over a thousand miles to collect silverware and gold beads from her friends for the purpose of securing the then enormous bail of $15,000 for the release of one Matthew Lyon, of Rutland, incarcerated for violation of the notorious sedition law.

For the first fifteen years of his life, the subject of this sketch lived on his father's farm at home, passing the uneventful days of a farmer boy, at work in summer, and at the district school in winter. At this age, however, he went to the Castleton (Vt.) Academy, where he fitted for the higher course of study which he subsequently pursued. He entered college at Middlebury, from which he was graduated with honors, in the medical course, in 1830.

He began the practice of medicine at Newark, N. J., where he achieved enough local success to make him ambitious for a broader field in which to try his talents and exercise his industry. Like other aspiring young men of his time, he cast longing eyes toward the new West, and finally resolved to take the trip and trust his fortunes with the destinies of Chicago, where he arrived in August, 1835. He married Miss Louisa M. Gifford, of Elgin, in 1837, a lady who proved to be a woman of most sterling character, and whose long life of usefulnesss has but recently closed in death. The couple were blessed with six children, three of whom survive—a daughter, wife of Mr. S.

E. Loring, and two sons, Charles, an artist, now in Italy, and Louis, a professor in the Chicago University.

Dr. Dyer, upon his arrival, was appointed surgeon of old Fort Dearborn, and from that time his practice grew to such an extent, that in the course of a short time he had means to invest. With the infinite faith in the future that has characterized Chicago's pioneers, he purchased a large amount of real estate then outside of the corporation. Among other spots, once his property, is the lot now occupied by the " First National Bank Building," which he sold to the government for the old post-office, for the sum of $46,000.

In 1854 he had acquired a competence, and retired from the practice of his profession, determined to pass the remainder of his life quietly, in the care of his considerable property.

Dr. Dyer was a Democrat when he first came to Chicago, and was elected by the Legislature to the office of Judge of the Probate Court of Cook county, in 1837. He soon after became a leading Abolitionist, and supported Birney for President in 1840. There were then very few Liberty party men, as they were called, in Illinois; but they had an "underground railroad," and many of the passengers called upon Dr. Dyer and the late James H. Collins, who were understood to be the proprietors, in passing through from the South to the land of freedom, in Canada. While these men stopped with the Doctor, he tried to make them useful by setting them to work; but he said they were more fond of preaching, than cutting and splitting wood. Dr. Dyer used to carry a large ebony, gold-headed cane, now in the collection of the Chicago Historical Society, which was presented to him by his admirers, as it was said, for enlightening a slave-catcher after the manner in which Minerva was freed from the skull of Jupiter. The Doctor was very proud of this token, which he regarded as Jacob's staff for freedom. About the time he received this present, say in 1846, a runaway slave was arrested and taken before the late Justice Kercheval, a native of Kentucky, who had issued a warrant for his arrest, under the old fugitive slave law. Mr. Collins appeard for the defence and moved to quash the writ, which was done. While new papers were being prepared for the re-arrest of the slave, Dr. Dyer was left alone with the handcuffed slave for a moment. He struck off the irons and bade the man jump for dear life. In a moment the others returned and, on their inquiring for the slave, Dr. Dyer said: "He has sunk into the bosom of the community." At an anti-slavery convention, held in Chicago, it was resolved to start an abolition paper in Washington. Dr. Dyer was made chairman of the committee, and selected Bailey as editor, with Whittier and Phelps as assistants. This was the beginning of the *National Era*.

In 1863 President Lincoln appointed him Judge of the Mixed Court for the Suppression of the African Slave Trade, an international tribunal, holding its sessions in Sierra Leone. In consequence of this very appropriate honor, he spent two years abroad, when not in Africa, traveling quietly with his family in Switzerland, Germany, and Italy. He chanced to be in Rome when the sad news of the death of Lincoln fell upon the world, and he was chosen to make an address in memory of his dead friend. In religious belief the Doctor was a follower of Swedenborg, having embraced the tenets of the Scandinavian philosopher in 1854. Soon after this, he and his wife, in connection with the Hon. and Mrs. J. Y. Scammon and Mr. and Mrs. J. E. Wheeler, founded the New Jerusalem Society of this city. The great fire of 1871, and the panic, greatly straitened Dr. Dyer's circumstances, and his ready pecuniary means were nearly exhausted at the time of his death. He was a very peculiar man, *sui generis* in the fullest sense of that expression. No one who has ever known him well, could ever forget him. He loved a joke so well that, if he had had a chance, like Hood, he would have made his pun even to his last breath. It is impossible to do his varied character justice within the limits of a brief notice like this, but he will always be remembered in the Northwest as one of those vigorous men who braved the perils of the old frontier to build an empire upon a wilderness, and who held the most profound political convictions, not for personal glory, but that he might fulfil the promise of American freedom, and raise a fallen race to the fold of humanity.

Charles Gifford Dyer, son of Dr. Charles Volney

Dyer, was born in Chicago in 1845. Educated at Lake Forest, until he entered the Naval Academy, then at Newport. Shortly before finishing his studies there, a strong inclination for painting, and the urgent desire of his family, led him to resign. He then pursued the study of art in Dresden and Munich, but at the end of two years abandoned it and returned to Chicago. After convincing himself that commerce was not his vocation, by five years of repugnant labor, he again devoted himself to the study of painting with such persistency as his health, now greatly impaired by the hardships and disgusts of his commercial venture, allowed. To restore his health, he was obliged to travel extensively in Italy, Egypt, and the East. Much of his work in his profession was done at Munich, in 1876. He finally abandoned Munich for a time, and studied to great advantage in the *atelier* of Jaquesson de la Chevreuse at Paris. In the course of his study, Venice and its great monuments attracted him, and the best known work which he has done is to be found in America, and connects itself with St. Mark's, Venice. A picture by him, entitled "A German Student," attracted much attention in the Royal Academy at London, and at Munich, where he now has his atelier. His works are scattered among private collections in England and America.

Louis Dyer, son of Dr. Charles Volney Dyer, was born in Chicago in 1851. Educated in Chicago—at the Chateau de Lancy, near Geneva, Switzerland—at

St. Amand-Montroud (Cher) France—at the University of Munich, and finally graduated from Harvard in 1874. After leaving Harvard L.D. he matriculated at Balliol College, Oxford, England, where he took his degree in July, 1878, and was for one year Taylorian scholar. In September of the same year, he was appointed tutor in Greek, by the corporation of Harvard College, Mass., and at the expiration of the term of this appointment he was in 1881 appointed assistant professor of Latin and Greek, at Harvard College, where he now teaches. Professor Dyer not only takes high rank as a scholar, but is also a poet and a man of many accomplishments.

Olin Gideon Dyer, M.D., the youngest son of Gideon Dyer, was born in Clarendon, Vt., December 5th, 1822. From force of circumstances, he was unable to pursue a classical course of study, but nevertheless he succeeded in obtaining a good common school education. At an early age, becoming interested in the subject of medicine, he commenced to study under the guidance and tuition of the late Dr. Moses H. Ranney, who afterwards became distinguished in New York as a specialist in mental disease, and graduated at the Castleton Medical College—then one of the most flourishing medical institutions of the day—with the highest honors in June, 1844. He commenced the practice of his profession during the succeeding year in Lexington, Ohio, where he remained but one year, when he returned to Vermont. In August, 1846, he married Annah Gaines Holt, of Pittsfield, and immediately located in Salisbury, where he remained in active practice for five years. At the expiration of this time, to wit, September, 1851, at the earnest solicitation of the late Dr. A. G. Dana, he removed to Brandon, Vt., to become his associate in practice. Owing however to the ill health of Dr. Dana, the partnership terminated in two years, by his voluntary withdrawal, since which time, Dr. Dyer has occupied the field against all competitors, with signal ability and success, until the present time.

At the close of the war he received the unsolicited appointment of examining surgeon for pensions, which office he still holds. As a man, Dr. Dyer is held in the highest esteem and is above reproach, while, as a physician, he possesses in a rare degree that intuitive knowledge of disease which has rendered him so remarkably skilful and successful that he is regarded, by all, as the leading medical man in Brandon and vicinity.

The Rev. Palmer Dyer, an estimable Episcopal clergyman, was a son of Edward Dyer, of Rutland, Vt., and was born October 24th, 1798. He graduated at Union College in 1820, studied theology, and was ordained deacon by Bishop Brownell, of Connecticut. His useful life came to an untimely end by drowning in the Ausable River, August 1st, 1844, while he was endeavoring to save the life of a lady, who had slipped on a narrow bridge, and was in great danger. She was saved, and her noble rescuer perished.[×]

There are many descendants of Charles Dyre, the youngest son of William and Mary Dyre, living in various parts of Rhode Isand. He had two daughters and five sons: Mary, Eliza, Samuel, John, William, Thomas, and Charles. He died in 1727. The following sketches are of some of his descendants:

Benjamin Dyer, M.D., was born in Cranston, Rhode Island, July 8th, 1768. His father was the son of Charles Dyer, Jr., who married Abigail Williams, daughter of Thomas Williams and great-granddaughter of Roger Williams. Charles Dyer, 1st, of Providence came from Dartmouth, Bristol county, Massachusetts, and purchased the farm now known as " Cabbage Neck," Cranston, his deed being dated July 25, 1712. He married Mary Lapham, and they had seven children. The subject of this sketch received such education as the schools of his day afforded, and at an early age entered upon the study of medicine, under the direction of Nathan Truman, who was then one of the prominent physicians of Providence. Dr. Dyer engaged successfully in the practice of medicine, and became associated with his brother, Charles Dyer, in the drug business, in Providence, in which he continued until his death. He pursued his profession with great assiduity for a period of twenty years, and then relinquished his professional business, in order to devote his time to mercantile and manufacturing pursuits, and to the improvement of the extensive landed property belonging to himself, and the firm of which he was a partner. His apothecary business rapidly increased, and the firm became large dealers in chemicals and dyestuffs, from the sale of which a handsome fortune was realized. In 1816, in company with his brother Charles, Benjamin Hoppin, Stephen Waterman and others, he became interested in the purchase and improvement of lands on the west side of the river, which then belonged to the Field estate. They filled in and laid out Dyer, Dorrance, Eddy and other streets in that vicinity, and built wharves and store-houses, investing immense sums of money in the enterprise, with great advantage to the city, and serious loss to themselves. Dr. Dyer was also one of the originators of the Providence Dyeing, Bleaching and Calendering Company and of the Phœnix Iron Foundry. In 1824 he built the Dyer block, on Broad street. He also built the steam-mill on Eddy Street, now owned by Amos D. Smith & Co. He owned a large tract of land in Cranston, now Elmwood, between Broad and Greenwich streets, where he had a fine country residence for a summer home, and where he was interested in various agricultural enterprises. At one time he devoted considerable attention to the raising of currants for the manufacture of wine, and also to silk growing on his own premises Some of his friends still remember seeing him at an agricultural fair, dressed in a beautiful suit of silk made from products of his own culture. His energy and enterprising spirit, gave vigor and promised success to every undertaking, and the deep interest which he continually manifested in the public welfare, caused him to be regarded as one of the most useful citizens of his day. As a physician he was skilful and devoted to his profession. He often sacrificed time, money, and professional services for the relief of the suffering poor. As an instance of his benevolence, it is said that, during his professional career, he was attending a poor woman who was dangerously ill with typhoid fever, and seeing that she could not recover if she remained in the unwholesome district where she lived, he removed her to his own house, and cared for her until her health was restored. He was noted for his sociability, hospitality, and benevolence. Dr. Dyer was always one of the first to promote all practical charities and public institutions for good. Being of modest and very retiring disposition, he never accepted official positions. He was a member of a sect known as Sandemanians, of which it is said there is but one society in this country, at Danbury, Connecticut. The few members of the society in Providence met with him and his family at his house, and he conducted the religious services. At his death, which occurred May 15, 1831, his family became members of the Beneficent Congregational Church.

Hon. Elisha Dyer, ex-Governor of Rhode Island, son of Elisha and Frances (Jones) Dyer, was born in Providence, Rhode Island, July 20, 1811. He is a lineal descendant of William and Mary Dyre. Their grandson, John, married Freelove Williams, a great-granddaughter of Roger Williams, and John Dyer's son, Anthony, was the grandfather of the subject of this sketch. Governor Dyer's mother was a daughter of Esther Jones, a great-granddaughter of Mary Bernon, who was a daughter of Gabriel Bernon, a Huguenot, and a refugee from La Rochelle, France. Gabriel Bernon was a merchant of an ancient and honorable family of Rochelle, where he was born April 6, 1644. Governor Dyer enjoyed superior educational advantages. He received early and careful training in private schools in Providence, spent a short time at Benjamin Greene's boarding-school, at Black Hill, in Plainfield, Connecticut, and was prepared for college in Roswell C. Smith's school, in Providence, from which he entered Brown University, September 7, 1825, at the age of fourteen. He gradated from that institution September 2, 1829, and September 1st of the same year entered the store of Elisha Dyer & Co., commission merchants, No. 5 West Water street, Providence, where he served in a clerical capacity until April 1, 1831, when, Mr. Cary Dunn having retired from the firm to engage in business in New York, young Dyer became the junior partner. On the 8th of October, 1838, he married Anna Jones Hoppin, daughter of Thomas C. Hoppin, Esq. By this marriage there were seven children, four of whom —Elisha, Anna Jones, Gabriel Bernon, and William Jones—are now living. In early life Governor Dyer became identified with various public interests, and has always taken an active part in promoting useful enterprises and social reforms. On the 23d of September, 1833, he was tendered the appointment of vice-consul of the two Sicilies, which honor he declined. About this time he became a strong temperance man, and by earnest persuasion prevailed on his father to give up the sale of intoxicating liquors, then a large and profitable part of their business, which course, as was expected, proved very damaging to their trade. This incident illustrates a strong characteristic of Governor Dyer's life. He is a man of high moral principle, and has always been true to his convictions. On the 30th of September, 1835, he became a member of the Rhode Island Society for the Encouragement of Domestic Industry, of which he subsequently served as secretary, member of the Auditing Committee, and president, and from 1859 to 1878 was an honorary member, and a member of the Standing Committee. Perhaps no one has done more for the success of this society than Governor Dyer. He worked earnestly, both at home and abroad, to promote its usefulness. He visited agricultural colleges in Europe, and obtained valuable statistics and information for the society in this country, while travelling for his health. In 1835 his father built the Dyerville Mill, in North Providence, and established the Dyerville Manufacturing Company, for the manufacture of cotton cloth. Mr. Dyer became the agent of this company, in which position he served until the death of his father, in 1854, when he became the sole owner of the property, and continued the business until 1867, when, on account of failing health, being obliged to retire from business, he sold the mill. During his business career, he was prominently identified with many of the commercial interests of the city. For many years he was a member and director of the Providence Athenæum, a director of the Providence Young Men's Bible Society, of which he was president in 1843, and was a member of the Providence Dispensary, being among the most generous in caring for the poor and unfortunate. He became a member of the Rhode Island Historical Society in 1837, and was one of the Board of Trustees, from September 10, 1845, until the abolishment of the same in 1848. In politics Governor Dyer was formerly an old line Whig, and has been identified with the Republican party since its organization. He was a delegate to the Whig Convention at South Kingstown, Rhode Island, October 31, 1839, and secretary of the same; and a delegate to the Whig Jubilee and Festival at Niblo's, New York, in November, 1839. He was chairman and first vice-president of the Young Men's Whig Convention at Providence, April 2, 1840. He was a delegate to the Young Men's Whig Convention at Baltimore, May 3, 1840, of which he was chairman, and at that time addressed ten thousand people in Monument Square, Baltimore. On the 27th of June, 1840, he was elected Adjutant-General of Rhode Island, and re-elected for five successive years, in which capacity he rendered very efficient service, being on active duty under Governor Samuel W. King, constantly, from April 3d to July 21st, 1842, having almost entire charge of the plans and movements of the State government during the "Dorr War." He served as a member of the Providence School Committee, from January 3, 1843, to June 6, 1854, when he resigned. In 1851 he was nominated for Mayor of Providence by the Temperance party, and defeated by a small majority.

On the 4th of April, 1853, he was nominated for State Senator, but not elected. He was president of the Exchange Bank of Providence at the time it became a national bank, and served as a director of the same from 1837 to 1879; was elected a director of the Union Bank of Providence, September 2, 1845, and became a director of the Providence and Washington Insurance Company in January, 1850, but soon afterward resigned. He was second vice-president of the Rhode Island Art Association in 1853. In 1854 he became an annual member of the United States Agricultural Society, and in 1857 a life member and vice-president of the same. He was also a member of the Windham County (Connecticut) Agricultural Society. In August, 1855, he became a member of the American Association of Arts and Sciences. He was a member of the Butler Hospital Corporation, and trustee of the same from January 23, 1856, to June 5, 1857, when he resigned; was vice-president of the Lake Erie Monument Association; president of the Young Men's Christian Association from May 12,

1857, to April 12, 1858; honorary member of Franklin Lyceum in 1858, and of the Providence Association of Mechanics and Manufacturers in 1860. On the 10th of March, 1853, he was a delegate to the Whig State Convention, and secretary of the same, and at the same time was chairman of the Eastern District Convention. In 1857 he was elected Governor of Rhode Island, and re-elected in 1858, and declined in favor of Hon. Thomas G. Turner, in May, 1859. Concerning his administration as Governor, the Providence *Post*, a leading Democratic paper, which was opposed to him, thus referred to him on the 7th of March, 1859: "It is proper to say that his retirement is wholly voluntary. It is not often that men thus voluntarily decline an honorable office, and especially when the office may be used as a stepping-stone to others of still greater value and importance. . . . We have from the first looked upon him as an honorable, high-minded opponent, and a straightforward, conscientious man; and candor compels us to say, that he has never failed to reach the standard we set up for him. His abilities have been equal to his official duties, and his integrity has been equal, so far as we know or suspect, to every assault which the intrigues of professed friends have made upon it. He retires from an office which he did not seek, wholly unscathed, and wholly uncontaminated with the slime which too often clings to men who dispense official favors." Governor Dyer was made a director of Swan Point Cemetery, February 7, 1860. He was one of the founders of the Providence Aid

Society, and was one of its board of managers from November 16, 1855, to October 1, 1859. On the 8th of November, 1849, he was elected an honorary member of the Rhode Island Horticultural Society, and one of the Committee on Finance, in 1854. Governor Dyer has taken a prominent part in military matters. He joined the First Light Infantry Company, of Providence, in 1838, was made an honorary member of the Newport Artillery Company in 1858, and an honorary member of the Providence Marine Corps of Artillery in 1859. During the civil war, he exhibited in various ways his patriotic devotion to the cause of his country. On the 25th of September, 1861, he was chosen captain of the Tenth Ward Drill Company, of Providence, and May 26, 1862, his son Elisha having been disabled and prevented from continuing in the service, Governor Dyer felt it his duty to volunteer himself, and accordingly went to Washington, and served for three months as captain of Company B, Tenth regiment of Rhode Island Volunteers. This company was composed of about one hundred and twenty-five students from Brown University and the Providence High School. President Sears, of the University, allowed his students to enlist only on condition that Governor Dyer should go with them. He was a director of the Providence and Springfield Railroad, and has been among the first in projecting and promoting various railroad enterprises in the State. He was the originator of the Providence and Springfield Railroad, known at first as the Woonasquatucket Railroad, and was one of the first movers in the proposed Ponagansett Railroad. He drew the charter of the Narragansett Valley Railroad, and was one of its corporators. In 1851, he was a director of the Rhode Island Steamboat Company. The same year he served on a committee sent to Washington to secure the removal of the Providence post-office. In 1852, he was elected a trustee of the Firemen's Association, Gaspé Company, No. 9. He was at one time one of the directors of the Rhode Island Sportsman's Club. In 1863, he was a delegate from the Rhode Island Society for the Encouragement of Domestic Industry, to the International Agricultural Exhibition at Hamburg, in July of that year, and made an able report of the same. He was vice-president of the Roger Williams Monument Association, and chairman of the Executive Committee. On the 24th of September, 1869, he was elected president of the First National Musical Congress, in Music Hall, Boston, because of his musical ability, and his extensive acquaintance in musical circles. He was Commissioner for Rhode Island to the International Exhibition in London, in May, 1871, and made a valuable report of the same to the General Assembly. On the 20th of March, 1873, he was appointed Honorary Commissioner to the Vienna Exposition by President Grant, and while there, rendered very important service to the Commission, by reason of his large and varied experience, and excellent taste and judgment. His patriotic zeal led him to over-exert himself at the

Exposition, so much to the injury of his health, that since then, he has been obliged to retire altogether from public life and from business. He is a member of the Protestant Episcopal Church, being, with his family, connected with Grace Church, Providence. On the 8th of June, 1852, he was a delegate to the Diocesan Convention. Notwithstanding his active business and public career, Governor Dyer has been an invalid for the last thirty years, and very much of his work has been done under the burden of infirmity and suffering. Eighteen times he has crossed the Atlantic in search of health, and in 1854 visited Egypt. He has been in all the places of note on the usual routes of European travel, and, though travelling for health, always had his eyes open and note-book in hand, to glean whatever of value or interest he could preserve for others. He is an effective speaker, and has made a large number of public addresses on political, educational, musical, and miscellaneous subjects. In the Rhode Island *Schoolmaster*, of November, 1861, he published a charming sketch of his school-day experiences at "Black Hill," and in 1864, published a book, entitled "A Summer's Travel to Find a German Home." Governor Dyer is a man who might have succeeded in almost any chosen line of work that he had selected.

Colonel Elisha Dyer, Jr., chemist, son of Hon. Elisha and Anna Jones (Hoppin) Dyer, was born in Providence, Rhode Island, November 29, 1839. After attending the public schools of the city, and the school of Lyon and Frieze, he entered Brown University in 1856, taking a partial course. In 1858 he went to Germany, and entered the University of Giessen, where he graduated August 20, 1860, taking the degree of Doctor of Philosophy, having pursued his studies part of the time at Freiberg, in Saxony. He returned home in the autumn of 1860, and at the commencement of the civil war started for Washington, D. C., April 18, 1861, as fourth sergeant of Captain Tompkins's Battery of Rhode Island Light Artillery, being one of the first volunteers enlisted in the State, in response to the call for three months men. While in charge of unloading the battery at Easton, Pennsylvania, he received an injury which nearly disabled him, and, persisting in continuing with his company, was overcome by the heat a few days later, and sent home by order of the surgeon. He has never fully recovered from the shock and exposure which he then experienced. In 1862 he was re-elected lieutenant of the Marine Artillery, one of the oldest and finest military organizations in the State, having held a position on its staff before his enlistment for the war. In May of the same year the battery again enlisted for three months, but Lieutenant Dyer, who had volunteered, was rejected from service by the surgeon, on the ground of his previous disability. Governor Sprague at once appointed him major, and, with Lieutenant-Colonel George H. Smith, detailed him to recruit and drill men for the battery, which he continued to do for the remainder of the year. The following year Governor James Y. Smith appointed him colonel on his staff, in which position he served for three years. In 1867, the Marine Artillery Company was reorganized, and Colonel Dyer entered its ranks as corporal. In 1869 he was elected lieutenant-colonel commanding the company, which office he resigned after two years, and one year thereafter was again made commander for another term of two years. In 1875, under the new militia law, all the artillery of the State was consolidated, and Colonel Dyer was elected to the command of the battalion. At the same time, he was appointed a member of the Board of Examiners of Officers of the State Militia, which position he held until 1878. In 1877 he was elected to the State Senate from North Kingstown, and during his term of service was a member of the Judiciary Committee, and chairman of the Committee on Militia. In 1878 he was appointed, by a convention of militia officers, one of the commission to report a new militia law to the General Assembly. He was appointed by Governor Van Zandt, and served as a member of the Joint Select Committee on the reception of President Hayes and cabinet, in 1877. He was also appointed for five years a member of the State Board of Health, for Washington county, in 1878. In 1881 he was elected a Representative to the General Assembly, from the Fourth ward of Providence. He has been one of the directors of the Union Bank and of the Union Savings Bank of Providence since 1870. For several years he was one of the Finance Committee of the Rhode Island Society for the Encouragement of Domestic Industry. His chosen profession is that of a chemist, and he has been engaged from time to time in various manufacturing interests, but of late years has been very busily occupied with the care and management of the estate of his father. He married November 26, 1861, Nancy Anthony, daughter of William and Mary B. (Anthony) Viall, of Providence. They have three sons—Elisha, George R., and H. Anthony. Throughout his life Colonel Dyer has labored earnestly for the best interests of mankind, and enjoys the satisfaction of having done worthily whatever he has undertaken.

[*From the Manchester (England) Examiner and Times, May 9th,* 1871.]

THE LATE MR. J. C. DYER.

IN our obituary on Saturday, we announced the death of one whose name, almost forgotten now, except as matter of history, was, a generation ago, known as one of the foremost in the ranks of the advanced Liberal party in Lancashire. Mr. Joseph Chessborough Dyer, of Burnage, who died at his son's residence at Henbury, near Macclesfield, on Wednesday last, was from 1816, when he settled in Manchester, till after the settlement of the corn-law question, one of the most prominent leaders of popular movements in the district, besides holding an important place in the scientific development of the cotton industry, which has elevated Lancashire into the foremost rank among English counties. Mr. Dyer's democratic leanings may be said to have been hereditary, for his father was a leader in the struggle for American independence, and is said to have been one of the signatories of the world-famous documents in which the rights of the colonists were declared and asserted. The subject of our sketch, however, was especially proud of his English descent, and being born in 1780, three years before the acknowledgment by England of the independence of the United States, although the place of his birth was Stonington, in Connecticut, he was able to claim that he was "born an Englishman." Upon this point, he was so interested that he obtained the opinion of counsel (Scarletts), which was distinctly in his favor. He received the usual education of his class; and on attaining manhood, established himself in Boston, as a merchant importing British goods, and in that capacity frequently visited England, in the early part of the century. In 1811, in consequence of the disturbances between the mother country and the States, Jefferson's non-intercourse act was passed, with the effect of ruining the American trade in English goods. Mr. Dyer, thereupon, removed at once to London. In 1811, he married Miss Eliza Jones, daughter of Mr. Somersett Jones, of Gower street, London, and Brand House, Somersetshire, a nephew of Sir William Jones, the well known Indian scholar. After a brief residence in Birmingham, where he projected the *North*

American Review, and, along with Mr. Tudor, prepared the first three numbers of the magazine, he settled in Manchester, and in this town or its immediate neighborhood, he lived till 1864. For two years afterwards he lived with his son, Mr. F. N. Dyer, at Whaley Bridge, and since then, till the time of his death, at that gentleman's seat at Henbury. Mr. Dyer, shortly after his settlement in Manchester, by the adaptation of several useful American inventions, gave a great impetus to the cotton trade, which was then rapidly developing in this district. Wheeler, in his "History of Manchester," after speaking of the inventions of the mule and throstle spinning, says: "Two other important inventions have yet to be named—the fly frame, introduced about 1817, which supersedes the roving frame for middle and lower numbers (of yarns); and the tube frame, which roves much faster than fly, but only for low numbers. Mr. Dyer, of this town, introduced them from America, and in 1825 and 1829 took out patents." So rapidly was the importance of these inventions recognized, that it is said that in a few years nearly 1,000 improved frames were in operation in the mills of the cotton district. Mr. Dyer was the founder of one of the largest firms of machinists in Manchester. Mr. Dyer was a director of the Bank of Manchester, in which he was a considerable shareholder. By its stoppage, during the joint-stock bank panic between 1836 and 1842, he suffered severe pecuniary losses. Even while engaged in business pursuits, Mr. Dyer was an active politician; but after his retirement, many of his best years were given up almost wholly to the advancement of the political and social condition of the people. His public services embraced a very wide range. In 1824 he was one of the projectors of the Royal Institution of Manchester, and a liberal subscriber. He was, also, about the same time, one of the first to subscribe towards the formation of the Manchester Mechanics' Institute. He was a moving spirit in the counsels of those advanced Radicals, through whose action, chiefly, Manchester obtained the position of a borough, returning two members under the reform bill of 1832, and subsequently he was equally active in the movement for obtaining a charter of incorporation for the city. The prominent position which, at this time, Mr. Dyer held in Manchester politics may be judged of from the fact that in 1830, along with Mr. Mark Phillips (subsequently one of the first members for Manchester) and Mr. Alexander Kay, he was nominated at a public meeting in the Town Hall, to bear the congratulations of the citizens to the people of Paris, on the success of the revolution of July. The Manchester delegates were received at the Hôtel de Ville, and a public banquet was given in their honor. Mr. Dyer was chairman of the Manchester branch of the old Reform League, and took a leading part in all the agitations preceding the passage of the act of 1832. The influence which Mr. Dyer then obtained, was used to good purpose at the first election for the new-created borough. Mr. C. Poulett Thompson, who was nominated along with Mr. Mark Philips as a Liberal candidate, being unable, in consequence of his candidature for Dover, to attend personally to his canvass here, was represented by Mr. Dyer, who had the satisfaction of returning his candidate. Mr. Dyer was one of the first, and remained to the successful close of its labors, one of the leading members of the Anti-Corn-Law League. He also took an active part in most of the public measures which engaged attention from 1820 to 1850. Shortly after the latter date, being now more than 70 years old, he retired, almost entirely, from participation in public business, in which, however, he preserved till the last a keen interest. In 1818, Mr. Dyer was elected a member of the Manchester Literary and Philosophical Society, of which he was for many years a vice-president. He contributed many papers, which occupy an honored place in its records, and is notable as the only member who was ever allowed to address the society on a semi-political question. This was in a paper written during the height of the corn-law agitation, to combat the notion, founded on Goldsmith's couplet, that the growth of large towns and the increase of wealth indicated the decay of the nation. As a pamphleteer, Mr. Dyer was, also, very prolific, and many of his papers on the political and social questions of his time were of more than passing value. We are informed that he has left behind him, in manuscript, a History of his Own Times, a treatise on health and longevity, and an autobiography extending to the period of his marriage. The funeral took place on Saturday, and in accordance with Mr. Dyer's express desire, frequently reiterated during his last illness, was strictly private. His remains were interred in Rusholme Road Cemetery.

In the year 1632, Thomas Dyer, and his wife, arrived in Boston, from Shepton Mallett, in Somersetshire, England. Thomas Dyer married Agnes Reed, who was born in Butley, two miles from the beautiful town of Glastonbury, in Somersetshire. Shepton Mallett is a large manufacturing town; it carries on an extensive manufactory of knit stockings and woolen goods. These, with its market-cross, erected in 1500— a curious structure, supported by columns and adorned with sculpture—are its principal attractions. Thomas Dyer was a cloth manufacturer; but whether he pursued that line of business in this country, I have not been able to ascertain. He settled in Weymouth, in Massachusetts. His wife died in 1667, leaving eight children, five sons and three daughters. He was made freeman in 1644—was chosen Representative in 1646, —in 1650 was appointed deacon of the church. He died in 1676, leaving a " good estate." From him are descended very many of the name in this country, but it is not known that there was any relationship between him and *William Dyre*. Prominent among his descendants, is Colonel Eliphalet Dyer of Wyndham, Connecticut, who was the great-grandson of Thomas Dyer. He was born September 14th, 1721, and married Huldah Bowen, daughter of Colonel Jabez Bowen, of Providence, Rhode Island. He commenced the practice of law when nineteen years of age, and graduated at Yale College in 1740, where in 1787 he was made LL.D.; from 1745 to 1762 he was representative to the General Court. He commanded a Connecticut regiment during the French war—was elected a member of the council in 1762 and a delegate to the Stamp Act Congress in 1765—went to England, in 1763, as agent of the Susquehanna Company, and was also a delegate to Congress in 1774, and, excepting 1779, held during the war, a seat in that body. He had much to do with framing the constitution of the United States. He was appointed a judge of the Supreme Court in 1765, and from 1789 to 1793 was chief justice. He died in May, 1807. His daughter Amelia married Colonel Joseph Trumbull, oldest son of Governor Trumbull. The following ludicrous story is often alluded to:

"Rome had her geese and Pomfret her wolf, but Windham had her frogs. Here on the historic green, in sight of the pond where it occurred, the episode of the frogs assumes a very different aspect from that given it by the Rev. Hugh Peters in his humorous 'History of Connecticut.' It was on the night of June 17, 1754, that the gruesome, grotesque circumstance occurred. The green was as fresh and vivid in coloring, the elms arched as gracefully, the stream from the pond broke over its barriers, and flowed away under the rustic bridge as murmuringly then, as now, but in the minds of the people there was sad foreboding, and expectation of the momentary outbreak of a savage foe. It was the eve of one of the bloodiest of the French and Indian wars. Windham county had special reason for fearing vengeance, since, in acquiring some parts of her recent Susquehanna purchase, the Indians were known to have been aggrieved and wronged. Goodman White's negro slave, Pomp, was the first to experience the terrors of the night. Having lingered until a late hour beside a dusky Phyllis, in one of the outlying farmhouses, he at length started to return to the village, a Voudoo charm about his neck, and a horseshoe in his hand, as a protection against spooks. The night was still, misty, and intensely dark. Pomp went his way whistling, his fears equally divided between the insubstantial ghost, and the more material Mohawk. He had reached the green, when all at once a dire uproar burst upon him. Roar, bellow, gabble, shriek, splash, gurgle were combined, and the sounds came from everywhere at once—above, below, on this side and that, from field, and pond, and forest. To say that Pomp fled, and shrieked, and prayed, conveys no idea of the celerity of his flight, nor the intensity of his groans and supplications. But before he could reach the centre of the green, chamber windows were thrown open, nightcapped heads were thrust forth, and feminine shrieks, and the strong cries of men added to the uproar: many swooned; the stronger fled as they were to the village green, where they huddled in a little group, every eye upturned to see through the murky gloom the glory of the opening heavens, and the awful visage of the descending Judge. In that company, not one but believed that the last great day was at hand.

But the levin-stroke of judgment failed to come, and soon the thought came to the stronger minds, that the uproar was of terrestrial origin, and attributable to savage foes. Peering into the darkness, and shrinking from the possible deadly tomahawk, they waited and watched. At length they heard, amid the general babel, distinct articulations which gradually resolved themselves into the names of two of Windham's most prominent citizens—Colonel Dyer, the agent, and Squire Elderkin, one of the trustees of the Susquehanna Company. 'We'll have Colonel Dyer! We'll have Colonel Dyer! We'll have Colonel Dyer!' the mysterious voices declared; and 'Elderkin too!' 'Elderkin too!' 'Elderkin too!' an equally mysterious chorus repeated; not a person but trembled for the fate of those two strong pillars of the commonwealth. The words 'Tete,' 'Tete,' which followed, were construed as meaning that the investing force was disposed to treat, but as nothing could be done in the darkness, the affrighted people contented themselves with placing a line of sentries around the town, and then withdrew to their homes. In the morning no savage army appeared, nor was any cause of the strange voices of the night discoverable, and the occurrence would, no doubt, have been added to the long list of supernatural events detailed in Cotton Mather's Wonder-Book, had not Pomp, watering his master's horses at the pond next morning, discovered multitudes of frogs lying dead, and blackened in the water. Then it came as a revelation to the people of Windham, that an army of frogs, smitten with some deadly epidemic, or, perhaps attacked by some invading army, had produced the affrighting sounds. The revulsion of feeling, it is said, was great; the whole village assumed a sheepish air. Somehow, too, the story got abroad, and brought a ripple of laughter to the face of the whole county. Everybody was disposed to regard the experience of that terrible night as a rich joke. Gibes, puns, lampoons, ditties, proverbs were rained on the unfortunate Windhamites. Even the clergymen poked fun, as the following letter from the Rev. Mr. Stiles, of Woodstock, to his nephew, abundantly shows. It is dated at Woodstock, July 9, 1754, and proceeds:

"'If the late tragical tidings from Windham deserve credit, as doubtless they do, it will then concern the gentlemen of your Jurispritian order to be fortified against the croaks of Taurancan legions—legions terrible as the very wreck of matter and the crash of worlds. Antiquity relates that the elephant fears the mouse; a herd trembles at the crowing of a cock; but pray whence is it that the croaking of a bull-frog should so Belthazzarize a lawyer? How Dyerful the alarm made by these audacious long-winded croakers! I hope, sir, from the Dyerful reports from the frog-pond you will gain some instruction, as well as from the reports of my Lord Coke.'"

Even the aid of the Muses was invoked on this occasion, and a poem thirty verses long was written to describe the

"Fright which happen'd one night,
Caused by the bull-frog nation."

The following are two of the verses

"Lawyer Lucifer called up his crew,—
Dyer and Elderkin, you must come too;
Old Col. Dyer, you know well enough,
He had an old negro, his name was Cuff.

" 'Now, Massa,' says Cuff, 'I'm now glad enough
For what little comfort I have;
I make it, no doubt, my time is just out,
No longer shall I be a slave.' "

The five following articles are of interest to all bearing the name of Dyer. Much of the information contained in them is taken from Alexander Chalmers' Biographical Dictionary—London 1813.

Sir James Dyer, Dier, or Dyre, an eminent English lawyer, was descended from an ancient and honorable family in Somersetshire, of the same family with Sir Edward Dyer, the poet, who was fourth in descent from Sir James Dyer's great-grandfather. Sir James was the second son of Richard Dyer, Esq., of Wincalton and Round Hill, in Somersetshire, at the latter of which places he was born about the year 1512. Wood says he was a commoner of Broadgate Hall (now Pembroke College), Oxford, and that he left it without taking a degree, probably about 1530, when he went to the Middle Temple. Here he appears to have rendered himself conspicuous for learning and talents, as in 1552 he performed the office of autumnal reader to that society—a distinction which was at that time conferred only upon such as were eminent in their profession. He had, on May 10th preceding, been called to the degree of serjeant-at-law, and in the following November his abilities were rewarded with the post of King's serjeant. On the meeting of the last Parliament of Edward VI., 1552–3, Dyer was chosen Speaker of the House of Commons, (that office being considered in those days as peculiarly appropriate to lawyers of eminence,) and in this capacity, on Saturday afternoon, March 4, made "an ornate oration before the King." This is the only particular concerning this short Parliament, which sat only for one month, and the dissolution of which was quickly followed by the death of that excellent young Prince, whose successor, though in most respects she pursued measures totally opposite to those of his reign, continued the royal favor to Dyer, whom, October 19, 1553, she appointed one of her serjeants. In this office his name appears as one of the commissioners on the singular trial of Sir Nicholas Throckmorton, when his jury, with a freedom rarely exercised in that unhappy period, ventured to acquit the prisoner. Sir James's behavior on that occasion was not disgraced by any servile compliances with the views of the court; yet his regard for his own character was tempered with so much discretion as not to occasion any diminution of her Majesty's protection, for on May 20, 1557, being at that time Recorder of Cambridge and a knight, he was appointed a judge of the Common Pleas, whence, on April 23d of the next year, he was promoted to the Queen's Bench, where he sat (though of the Reformed religion) during the remainder of this reign as a puisne Judge. In the first year of Queen Elizabeth, on November 18, 1559, he returned to the Common Pleas, of which he was appointed in the following January chief justice—an office the functions of which he continued to exercise for more than twenty years, with eminent integrity, firmness, and ability. In the course of this long period, we find him assisting at the trial of Thomas Howard, Duke of Norfolk; on which occasion he opposed that unfortunate nobleman's petition to have a counsel assigned him, and with propriety, as the rigorous complexion of the law was at that time—it having been reserved for the milder spirit of a later age, to indulge prisoners in his unhappy situation with that privilege. In 1574 he exhibited a singular proof of probity, courage and talents, in the spirit with which he opposed the attempt of Sir John Conway to oppress a poor widow of Warwickshire, (that county being included in the circuit which he usually went,) by forcibly keeping possession of her farm; and in his reply to the articles preferred against him to the Privy Council, by certain justices of the peace, whom he had severely reprehended in public, at the assizes, for partiality and negligence in permitting so gross a violation of the law, and whom he had caused to be indicted for the same. What was the end of the dispute his biographer has not been able to discover, but thinks it reasonable to conclude that the firmness and ability of Dyer prevailed over the malice of his adversaries, as he experienced no diminution of the Queen's favor, but continued in the full exercise of his judicial functions, without any other memorable transaction that is known, down to his death, which happened at his seat of Great Stoughton (an estate purchased by himself), in the county of Huntingdon, March 24. 1582. at the age of seventy. Leaving no issue by his wife Margaret, daughter of Sir Maurice à Barrow, of Hampshire, a relict of the celebrated philologist, Sir Thomas Elyot, his estates at Stoughton and elsewhere, with his mansion-house at Charter House Church-yard, descended to Sir Richard Dyer, grandson of his elder brother, John. His will commences thus: "In the name of the Father, the Sonne, and the Holy Ghost, Amen. I, James Dyer, knight, chief justice of the Common Pleas, considering with myself the incertentye of this vaine and transitorye life, and the suddaine callinge awaie of us from the same, by deathe, and for the avoidinge of discorde and strife, that commonlie I see to ensue after the deathe of such as die intestate, about the trashe and pelfrye of this wicked worlde, being of perfect healthe and memorye (God be thanked), doe ordeyne and make this writinge withe myne owne hande, this my last will and testament, in manner and forme followinge."

He was buried at Stoughton; in the venerable church of which place is a handsome monument erected to his memory, with the following inscriptions:

Here lieth Sir James Deyer, Knight, sometimes Lord Chief Justice of the Common Pleas—and Dame Margaret, his wife: which Dame Margaret was here interr'd the six and twentieth day of August, 1560, and the said Sir James, upon the five and twentieth of March, 1582.

> Deyero tumulum quid statuis, Nepos ?
> Qui vivit volitaque ora per omnium.
> Exegit monumenta ipse perennia :
> In queis spirat adhuc : spirat in his themis
> Libertas, Pietas, Munificentia.
> En decreta, libros, vitam, obitum, senis!
> Eternas statuas! Vivat in his themis
> Libertas, Pietas, Munificentia.
> Eternas statuas has statuit sibi :
> Eternis statuis credite marmora!
> Patruo majori charissimo, ejusque
> Conjugi amantissimæ posuit Miles.
>
> RICHARDUS DEYER.

I am indebted to Professor Louis Dyer, of Harvard University, Cambridge, Mass., for a metrical translation of the Latin epitaph, which contains the spirit and significance of the original, admirably reproduced:

> A tomb for Dyer, thine uncle, wherefore raise ?
> Who lives, and quickened in the words men use
> Hath linked his memory to undying praise:
> While speech is speech his life he cannot lose,
> Whose righteousness must always be proclaimed
> When Largess, Freedom, Piety are named.

If thou his lasting monument wouldst see,
His thoughts, his deeds, his life and death revere—
And bid thy soul remember it is he
When Justice, Freedom, Piety appear ;
These he his deathless counterparts hath made,
Not here, in marble mimicry, portrayed.

Unto his very dear great Uncle, and that Uncle's very loving wife, the present Knight hath raised this tomb.

RICHARD DYER.

Sir James Dyer was the author of a large book of Reports, which were published after his decease, and have been highly esteemed for their succinctness and solidity. They were first printed in 1585, and have gone through many editions. That of 1688 is enriched by the marginal notes and references of Lord Chief Justice Treby, and bears the following title, literally translated from the French : "Reports of several select matters and resolutions of the reverend Judges and Sages of the Law, &c." That eminent lawyer, Sir Edward Coke, recommends to all students in the law these Reports, which he calls "the summary and fruitful observations of that famous and most reverend Judge and Sage of the Law, Sir James Dyer." They are, indeed, a valuable treasure to the profession. The best edition is that by John Vaillant, Esq., 1794, 3 vols., 8vo, with the life of the author from an original manuscript in the Inner Temple Library. It is entitled "Reports of cases in the reigns of Henry VIII., Edward VI., Queen Mary and Queen Elizabeth. Taken and collected by Sir James

Dyer, Knight—some time Justice of the Common Pleas." On the Inner Temple manuscripts of Law Reports, he signs his name James *Dier*. He left behind him, also, "A Reading upon the Statute of 32 Henry VIII., cap. 1, of Wills; and upon the 34th and 35th Henry VIII., cap. 5, for the explanation of the Statute," printed at London in 1648, 4to. By his will he bequeathed to his nephew, Richard Farwell, one of the editors of the "Reports," all his books of the law, "as well abridgments and reports of myne owne handwritinge, as other of the lawe," which expression seems to countenance the assertion of Cole, that he made an "Abridgment of the Law," but, as nothing of the kind has been discovered, it seems more reasonable to conclude that he wrote nothing except these "Reports," and the "Reading" above mentioned. By these performances, and by the services he did his country, he came fully up to the character which Camden has given him, of being ever distinguished by an equal and calm disposition, which rendered him in all cases a most upright judge, —as his penetration and learning made him a fit interpreter of the laws of his country. Not long after his death a book was published, entitled "A Remembrance of the Precious Vertues of the Right Honourable and Reverend Judge, Sir James Dier, Knight, Lord Cheefe Justice of the Common Pleas, who diseased at Great Stawghton, in Huntingdonshire, the 24th of Marche, Anno 1582. The reporte of George Whetstone, Gent. Imprinted at London by

John Charlewood, 4to. Dedicated to Sir Thomas Bromley, Lord Chancellor."

Collinson, in his "History of Somersetshire," says: "The manor and borough of Wincanton (formerly *Wincaleton*, from the River Cale, which rises near) has several hamlets on the outskirts. One is Barrow Common. Lands in the last-mentioned hamlet belonged to the priory of Taunton; after the dissolution of which, these lands, with the manor of Round Hill and the rectory of Wincanton, were sold to William Lord Stourton, whose son, Charles Lord Stourton, being attainted, the said lands came again to the Crown, and were sold in 1557, at thirty years' purchase, to *John Dier*." This was, undoubtedly, the elder brother of Sir James Dier.

Vaillant, in alluding to the various ways of spelling the name, says that "even at a much later period, orthography was very little attended to. The disputes between the commentators on Shakspeare, about our great poet's mode of writing his own name, are well known. It is not probable that Sir James Dyer's name was ever spelled *Deyer*, except upon his monument, where it was necessary, for the proper pronunciation of the Latin, to introduce an additional *e*.

One very important labor of Sir James Dyer was the union of Wales with England, by the abolition of the feudal jurisdiction of the eldest son of the King, under whose rule, fearful oppression was committed on the commonalty. Sir James rendered himself so beloved in Wales, by the accomplishment of the union, that, even to this day, "The Goat and Rose," his crest, is a common inn sign all over the principality. The portrait of Sir James Dyer is to be seen in the picture gallery of Chirk Castle, Denbighshire, near the beautiful vale of Llangollen, North Wales.

Sir Edward Dyer, a poet of the Elizabethan age, was of the same family with those of his name in Somersetshire, and was born, probably, about 1540. He was educated at Oxford, either in Balliol College or Broadgate Hall, where he discovered a propensity to poetry and polite literature, but left it without a degree, and travelled abroad. On his return, having the character of a well bred man, he was taken into the service of the court. He now obtained considerable celebrity as a poet, and was a contributor to the "Paradyce of Dainty Devyses" and "England's Helicon." He wrote "The Prayse of Nothing. Imprinted in London in Fleete-streate, beneath the Conduite, at the signe of St. John the Evangelist, by H. Jackson, 1585. 4to, black letter 15 leaves." Queen Elizabeth had a great respect for his abilities, and employed him in several embassies, particularly to Denmark in 1589; and on his return from thence conferred on him the Chancellorship of the Garter, on the death of Sir John Wolley, 1596, and at the same time she knighted him; but, like other courtiers, he occasionally suffered by her caprices. He was, at one time, reconciled to her, by her Majesty's being taught to believe that he was sinking to the grave, under the weight of her displeasure. Sir Edward partook of the credulity of the times, studied chemistry, and was thought to be a Rosicrucian. He was, at least, a dupe to the famous astrologers, Dr. Dee and Edward Kelly, of whom he has recorded that in Bohemia he saw them put base metal in a crucible, and after it was set on fire, and stirred with a stick of wood, it came forth, in great proportion, pure gold. He wrote pastoral odes and madrigals, some of which are in "England's Helicon," first published at the close of Queen Elizabeth's reign, and lately republished in the "Bibliographer." He wrote, also, a "Description of Friendship," a poem in the Ashmolean Museum, where, also, from Aubrey's manuscript, we learn that he spent an estate of £4,000 a year. There is a letter of his to Sir Christopher Hatton, dated October 9, 1572, in the Harleian MS., and another to the Earl of Leicester, dated May 22, 1586, in the Cottonian Collection, and some of his unpublished verses are in a MS. collection formerly belonging to Dr. Rawlinson, now in the Bodleian Library. There are two sonnets of Sir Edward Dyer's at the end of Sydney's "Arcadia," 1598, which are signed C. D. At the funeral of Sir Philip Sydney, he was one of the pall-bearers.

Sir Edward was an intimate friend of Sir Martin Frobisher, the celebrated English navigator; and with him, Sir Walter Raleigh, and another naval captain, carried the canopy over Queen Elizabeth, when she went to St. Paul's, to return thanks for the defeat of the Invincible Armada.

John Dyer, an English poet, was born in 1700, the second son of Robert Dyer, of Aberglasney, in Caermarthenshire, a solicitor of great capacity and note. He passed through Westminster school, under the care of Dr. Freind, and was then called home, to be instructed in his father's profession. His genius, however, led him a different way, for, besides his early taste for poetry, having a passion no less strong for the arts of design, he determined to make painting his profession. With this view, having studied awhile under his master, he became, as he tells his friend, an itinerant painter, and wandered about South Wales, and the parts adjacent, and about 1727 printed "Grongar Hill," a poem which Dr. Johnson says "is not very accurately written; but the scenes which it displays are so pleasing, the images which they raise, so welcome to the mind, and the reflections of the writer so consonant to the general sense or experience of mankind, that when it is once read, it will be read again." Being probably unsatisfied with his own proficiency, he made the tour of Italy, where, besides the usual study of the remains of antiquity and the works of the great masters, he frequently spent whole days in the country about Rome and Florence, sketching those picturesque prospects, with facility, and spirit. Images from hence naturally transferred themselves into his poetical compositions;

the principal beauties of the "Ruins of Rome" are, perhaps, of this kind, and the various landscapes in the "Fleece," have been particularly admired. On his return to England in 1740, he published the "Ruins of Rome," but soon found that he could not relish a town life, nor submit to the assiduity required in his profession. His talent, indeed, was rather for sketching than finishing, so he contentedly sat down in the country with his little fortune, painting now and then a portrait or a landscape, as his fancy led him. As his turn of mind was rather serious, and his conduct and behavior always irreproachable, he was advised by his friends to enter into orders; and it is presumed, though his education had not been regular, that he found no difficulty in obtaining them. He was ordained by the Bishop of Lincoln, and had a law degree conferred upon him. About the same time he married a lady of Coleshill, named Ensor, "whose grandmother," says he, "was a Shakspeare, descended from a brother of everybody's Shakspeare." His ecclesiastical provision was a long time but slender. His first patron, Mr. Harper, gave him, in 1741, Calthorp, in Leicestershire, of £80 a year, on which he lived ten years, and in April, 1757, exchanged it for Belchford, in Lincolnshire, of £75, which was given him by Lord Chancellor Hardwick, on the recommendation of a friend to virtue and the muses, Daniel Wray, Esq., one of the deputy tellers of the Exchequer, and a curator of the British Museum. For this gentleman Mr. Dyer seems to have entertained the sincerest regard. Mr. Dyer calls "good

Mr. Edwards," author of the "Canons of Criticism," his particular friend, and in Savage's poems are two epistles to Dyer; one of them in answer to the beautiful little poem which begins:

> "Have my friends in the town, in the gay busy town,
> Forgot such a man as John Dyer?"

His condition now began to mend. In the year 1752 Sir John Heathcote gave him Coningsby, of £140 a year, and in 1756, when he was LL.B., without any solicitation of his own, obtained for him, from the Chancellor, Kirkby-on-Bane, of £110. "I was glad of this," says Mr. Dyer in 1756, "on account of its nearness to me, though I think myself a loser by the exchange through the expense of the seal, dispensations, journeys, etc., and the charge of an old house, half of which I am going to pull down." The house, which is a very good one, owes much of its improvement to Mr. Dyer. His study, a little room with white walls, ascended by two steps, had a handsome window to the church-yard, which he stopped up, and opened a less, that gave him a full view of the fine church and castle at Gateshall, about a mile off, and of the road leading to it. He also improved the garden. In May, 1757, he was employed in rebuilding a large barn, which a late wind had blown down, and gathering materials for rebuilding above half the parsonage house at Kirby. "These," he says, "some years ago, I should have called trifles, but the evil days are come, and the lightest thing, even the grasshopper, is a burden upon the shoulders of the old and sickly."

He had then just published "The Fleece," his greatest poetical work, of which Dr. Johnson relates this ludicrous story: "Dodsley, the bookseller, was one day mentioning it to a critical visitor, with more expectation of success, than the other could easily admit. In the conversation the author's age was asked, and being represented as advanced in life, 'he will,' said the critic, 'be buried in woollen.'" He did not, indeed, long outlive that publication, nor long enjoy the increase of his preferments, for, a consumptive disorder, with which he had long struggled, carried him off at length, July 24, 1758.

Mr. Gough, who visited Coningsby, September 5, 1782, could find no memorial to him in the church. Mrs. Dyer, on her husband's decease, retired to her friends in Caermarthenshire. In 1756 they had four children living—three girls and a boy. Of these, Sarah died single. The son, a youth of the most amiable disposition, heir to his father's truly classical taste and to his uncle's estate of £300 or £400 a year in Suffolk, devoted the principal part of his time to travelling, and died in London, as he was preparing to set out on a tour to Italy in April, 1782, at the age of 32. This young gentleman's fortune was divided between two surviving sisters—one of them married to Alderman Hewitt, of Coventry; the other, Elizabeth, to the Rev. John Gaunt, of Birmingham. Mr. Dyer had some brothers, all of whom were dead in 1756, except one, who was a clergyman—yeoman of his Majesty's almonry—lived at Marylebone, and had then, a numerous family. Mr. Dyer's character as a writer has been fixed by three poems: "Grongar Hill," "The Ruins of Rome," and "The Fleece," in which a poetical imagination perfectly original, a natural simplicity connected with the true sublime and often productive of it, the warmest sentiments of benevolence and virtue, have been universally observed and admired. These pieces were published separately in his lifetime, but, after his death, collected in one volume, 8vo, 1761, with a short account of himself prefixed.

The poet, Wordsworth, has written so sweet a tribute "To the Poet, John Dyer," that I cannot resist quoting it:

"Bard of the Fleece, whose skilful genius made
That work a living landscape, fair and bright;
Nor hallow'd less with musical delight,
Than those soft scenes through which thy childhood stray'd,
Those southern tracts of Cambria, deep embay'd,
By green hills fenced, by ocean's murmur lull'd.
Though hasty Fame hath many a chaplet cull'd
For worthless brows, while, in the pensive shade
Of cold neglect, she leaves thy head ungraced,
Yet pure and powerful minds, hearts meek and still—
A grateful few—shall love thy modest lay
Long as the shepherd's bleating flock shall stray
O'er naked Snowdon's wide, aerial waste;
Long as the thrush shall pipe on Grongar Hill."

A modern critic compares the poet, John G. Whittier, to John Dyer, and says: "Unpretentious, yet an enthusiastic lover of nature in her several picturesque forms, nothing delights Whittier so much as to *dwell* on his favorite theme; and of all the poets since Dyer's time (the immortal author of 'Grongar Hill'), Whittier most reminds us of that exquisite delineator of natural scenery, who, while breaking out so enthusiastically, in the oft quoted lines, commencing

"'Ever charming, ever new,
When will the landscape tire the view?'"

makes us *feel* that John G. Whittier is Dyer's legitimate successor in song."

Samuel Dyer, a man of great learning, and the friend and associate of the literati of the last age, was born about 1725, and educated at Northampton, under Dr. Doddridge, and for some time, had the additional benefit of being instructed by the learned Dr. John Ward, professor of rhetoric, in Gresham College. He afterwards studied under Professor Hutcheson at Glasgow, and, to complete his education, his father, an eminent jeweller in London, sent him, by the advice of Dr. Chandler, to Leyden, where he remained two years. He became an excellent classical scholar, a great mathematician and natural philosopher; was well versed in the Hebrew, and a master of the Latin, Italian and French languages. Added to these endowments he was of a temper so mild, and in his conversation, so modest and unassuming, that he gained the attention and affection of all around him. In all questions of science, Dr. Johnson looked up to him; and, in his life of Dr. Watts, (where he calls him the "late learned Mr. Dyer",) has cited an observation of his, that Watts had confounded the idea of space, with that of *empty* space, and did not consider that, though space might be without matter, yet matter, being extended, could not be without space. Mr. Dyer appears to have been intended, by his early friends, for the ministry among the Dissenters, but discovered an averseness to the pastoral office, which Sir John Hawkins insinuates to have proceeded from an unfavorable change in his religious sentiments. Various literary schemes appear to have been suggested to him, none of which he undertook, except in 1758, the revisal of the English edition of Plutarch's Lives. In this he translated anew only the lives of Demetrius and Pericles. In 1759 he became a commissary in the army of Germany, and continued in that station to the end of the seven years' war, after which he returned to England, and, on the formation of the Literary Club (composed of Dr. Johnson and his friends) in 1764, he was the first member elected into that society, with whom he continued to associate and by whom he was highly esteemed to the time of his death, in September, 1772. From an excellent portrait of this gentleman, by Sir Joshua Reynolds, a mezzotinto print was scraped by his pupil Marchi, of which a copy was imposed upon the public as the portrait of John Dyer, the poet. Sir John Hawkins, in his Life of Johnson, has given a very unfavorable sketch of Mr. Dyer's character, representing him as an infidel and a sensualist. These charges, Mr. Malone, in a long note in his Life of Dryden, has minutely examined with a view to refute them, but in our opinion is more to be praised for the intention, than the execution of this desirable purpose. Sir John Hawkins seems to have drawn his facts from personal knowledge of Mr. Dyer. Mr. Malone does not pretend to this, and while he expresses a just indignation at Sir John's charging Mr. Dyer with infidelity, (supposing the charge to be false), he tells us that he himself had no means of knowing what Mr. Dyer's religious sentiments were. There is nothing conclusive, therefore, to be expected from one who is led, from whatever motive, to deny assertions without being able to prove that they are untrue. Mr. Malone is the first, if we mistake not, who himself asserted what he has not in the least attempted to prove, viz., that Dyer was the author of Junius's letters. This indeed he qualifies among his *errata*, by saying that Dyer was not the sole author, but the principal author. But even here he offers no kind of proof, nor, since the publication of the late edition of those celebrated letters, will it probably be thought that he had any to offer more worthy of attention than the conjectures which have ascribed these letters to a Boyd or a Wilmot.

George Dyer, an English author, born in a suburb of London, March 15, 1755, died in London, March 2, 1841. He was educated at Christ's Hospital, where he was an associate of Charles Lamb, and at Emmanuel

College, Cambridge, where he received the degree of bachelor in 1788. He was successively a teacher, tutor and a Baptist minister, residing most of the time either at Cambridge or Oxford, till, in 1792, he removed to London, where he was engaged as Parliamentary reporter, teacher and writer. In 1830 his eyesight failed him, and he at length became totally blind. He was a poet and frequent contributor to reviews, but is better known as a scholar and antiquary. He wrote "Complaints of the Poor"—a work on prison discipline, from personal examinations of the prisons in and about the metropolis. He edited two plays of Euripides and the Greek Testament; Valpy's Edition of the Classics, in 141 volumes; the "Poet's Fate," a poetical dialogue, inscribed to the Society for the Establishment of a Literary Fund; History of the University of Cambridge, and notices of its founders and eminent men, 1814.

In the Reminiscences of Henry Crabb Robinson, 1799, we find the following: "I became acquainted about this time with George Dyer. He was one of the best creatures morally that ever breathed. He was the son of a watchman in Wapping, and was put to a charity school by some pious Dissenting ladies. He afterwards went to Christ's Hospital, and from there was sent to Cambridge. He was a scholar, but to the end of his days (and he lived to be 85) was a bookseller's drudge. He led a life of literary labor in poverty. He made indexes, corrected the press, and occasionally gave lessons in Latin and Greek. When an undergraduate at Cambridge he became a hearer of Robert Robinson, and, consequently, a Unitarian. This closed the Church against him and he never had a fellowship. He became intimate with the Nashes, Fordhams, and Rutt, and was patronized by Wakefield and Mrs. Barbauld. He wrote one good book, the 'Life of Robert Robinson,' which I have heard Wordsworth mention as one of the best works of biography, in the language. Dyer also put his name to several volumes of poetry: but on his poems my friend Reid made an epigram, that I fear was thought just:

"'The world all say, my gentle Dyer,
Thy odes do very much want fire.
Repair the fault, my gentle Dyer,
And throw thy odes into the fire!'

"Dyer had the kindest heart, and simplest manners imaginable. It was literally the case with him that he would give away his last guinea. He was not sensible of any impropriety in wearing a dirty shirt or a ragged coat; and numerous are the tales told in illustration of his neglect of little every-day matters of comfort. He has asked a friend to breakfast with him, and given him coarse black tea, stale bread, salt butter, sour milk, and has had to run out to buy sugar. Yet, every one loved Dyer. One day Mrs. Barbauld said to me, 'Have you heard whom Lord Stanhope has made executor?' 'No! Your brother?' 'No, there would have been nothing in that. The very worst imaginable.' 'Oh'! then it is Bonaparte.' 'No—guess again.' 'George Dyer?' 'You are right. Lord Stanhope was clearly insane!' Dyer was one of six executors. Charles James Fox was another. The executors were also residuary legatees. Dyer was one of the first to declare that he rejected the legacy, and renounced the executorship. But the heir insisted on granting him a small annuity; his friends having before settled another on him, he was comparatively wealthy in his old age. Not many years before his death, he married his laundress, by the advice of his friends—a very worthy woman. He said to me, once, 'Mrs. Dyer is a woman of excellent natural sense, but she is not literary.' Dyer was blind, for a few years before his death. I used occasionally to go on a Sunday morning to read to him. At other times, a poor man used to render him that service for sixpence an hour. After he came to London, Dyer lived always in some very humble chambers in Clifford's Inn, Fleet street."

Thomas Noon Talfourd had a great regard for George Dyer and refers to his "simplicity of nature, not only unspotted by the world, but almost abstracted from it," and speaks of him as " breathing out, at the age of 85, the most blameless of lives, which began in a struggle, to end in a learned dream."

In Rose's Biographical Dictionary, I find an account of William Dyer, a Non-conformist ejected from his living of Cholesbury, in Buckinghamshire, in 1662. He turned Quaker in the latter part of his life, and died in 1696, aged 60, and was buried in Southwark. He wrote some sermons and theological tracts, much in the style of Bunyan. They were reprinted in 1671.

Thomas Henry Dyer, historian, was born May 1, 1804, in the parish of St. Dunstan in the East, in the city of London, and educated privately. He was engaged, during the earlier part of his life in a West India house, and after the ruin of Jamaica, in consequence of negro emancipation, adopted the profession of literature. Mr. Dyer travelled extensively on this Continent, and particularly studied the topography and antiquities of Rome, Athens, and Pompeii. He was presented in 1865 with the honorary degree of Doctor of Laws, by the University of St. Andrews. He published in 1850 a Life of Calvin, which was pirated in America; in 1861, a "History of Modern Europe," 4 vols.; in 1865, a "History of the City of Rome;" in 1867 an enlarged edition of "Pompeii;" in 1868, a "History of the Kings of Rome," and in 1873, "Ancient Athens;" besides many articles in the Classical Museum, in Dr. Smith's Dictionaries of Biography, and Geography, etc.

"From Mr. Frederick Nathaniel Dyer, of Macclesfield, England, I have received an interesting account of the family. Mr. Dyer is a lineal descendant of William and Mary Dyre, and has always resided in England. His father was born in Rhode Island. Mr. F. N. Dyer is a great-great-nephew of Sir William Jones, the distinguished oriental scholar, and is a man of culture, and literary tastes. He has had many opportunities of investigating the family history, and his information is undoubtedly accurate. He says, 'The Dyres were settled in Glastonbury, Somersetshire, before the Conquest. After the defeat of the Saxons at Senlac, near Hastings, Siward Dyre and his two sons, Siward Bearn and Wight, retired to Glastonbury, from whence they issued to make war on the Normans as occasion served, until, leaving their wives and children in charge of the monks, they joined Hereward in the famous Camp of Refuge. Siward Dyre (about 1036) was Earl of Northumbria, (earl being then an official title, and meaning military governor), and he is the Siward of Shakspeare's "Macbeth." He was descended from Alfred the Great, and I can prove, by legal proof, our descent from him and am able to bring such evidence to bear on the matter as will carry conviction to any sane mind.' Mr. Dyer also adds that there is no doubt of the descent of William and Mary Dyre, from Sir Richard Dyre, of Wincanton, Somersetshire, and gives the following account of the direct ancestors of the family: 'Sir Edward Dyre was probably a younger son, of no fortune. He was a poet and soldier. Queen Elizabeth appointed him Chancellor of the Garter. On her death, he retired from court, and disappeared from history, as no record of his death *is known.* His disappearance probably arose from some act repulsive to James the First. As Chancellor of the Garter, his loss would have been traced and noted. The probability is, that Huntingdonshire and Lincolnshire, being the stronghold of Puritanism, his espousal of these principles ignored him at court and by contemporaries. He may have been a proselyte and follower of Cromwell, and if so, probably went to Leyden, while his sons and daughters went to New England.' 'The last of the baronets of Great Staughton (descended from Sir Richard Dyre) died in 1776, and by a curious coincidence the representation of the baronetcy passed into the American branch of our race, in the year of the Declaration of Independence. The baronetcy has not been claimed, and it remains to be seen whether it ever will be.'"

From a "History of the Anglo-Saxons," by Sharon Turner, F.A.S., I find the following account of Siward Dyre, or *Digre*, as it was spelled in Anglo-Saxon times. "In 1054 while Macduff, the Thane of Fife, was exciting a formidable revolt in Scotland, Siward, by some called the Giant, from his large size, and whose sister had been Duncan's queen, conducted his Northumbrians against Macbeth. A furious conflict followed, in which thousands of both armies perished; but Siward, though he lost his son and nephew, defeated the usurper. He returned with great plunder, having made Malcolm king. The glory of a warrior was the felicity most precious to Siward. On his return to York, he felt that an internal disease was consuming his vitality, and he sighed for the funereal trophies of a field of battle. 'I feel disgraced that I should have survived so many combats, to perish now like a cow. Clothe me in my mail, fasten on my sword and give me my shield, and my battle-axe, that I may expire like a soldier!'"

On Siward's death in 1055, Tostig, the brother of Harold, was appointed Earl of Northumbria.

In "Camden's Remaines" it is stated that "when Siward, the martial Earl of Northumberland, understood that his son, whom he had sent against the Scotchmen, was slain, he demanded whether his wounds were in the fore part, or hinder part, of his body. When it was answered, 'In the fore part,' he replied, 'I am right glad; neither wish I any other death to me or mine.'"

Shakspeare has thus described this scene in Macbeth, act 5th, scene 7th, when the nobleman, Rosse, announced the death of young Siward to his father:

"*Rosse.* Your son, my lord, has paid a soldier's debt.
He only lived but till he was a man;
The which no sooner had his prowess confirmed
In the unshrinking station where he fought,
But like a man he died.
    Siward. Then he is dead?
    Rosse. Aye, and brought off the field; your cause of sorrow
Must not be measured by his worth, for then
It hath no end.
    Siward. Had he his hurts before?

> *Rosse.* Aye, on the front.
> *Siward.* Why, then, God's soldier be he!
> Had I as many sons as I have hairs,
> I would not wish them to a fairer death.
> And so his knell is knolled.
> *Malcolm.* He's worth more sorrow,
> And that I'll spend for him.
> *Siward.* He's worth no more;
> They say, he parted well, and paid his score;
> And so, God be with him!"

The first record of the family name which we find in Great Britain, is that of Dier or Dihenvyr, a saint who flourished in the sixth century, and founded the church of Bodffari, in Flintshire, North Wales. In the legend of St. Winifred, he is called Deiferus. In 1503 Jeffrey Dier was mayor of Carmarthen; and in 1514, Gwalter Dier filled the same office. This proves that the name was known in Wales before John Dyer, the poet, had so identified it with the Vale of Towy, through his much admired poem on Grongar Hill.

Henry II. established colonies of Flemish dyers in South Wales (Little England beyond Wales) as well as near Winchester and London, to introduce their trade into England. Many families descending from these men took their names from their trade, whence the multitude of Dyers who have no connection with the Dyres of Somersetshire.

In a manuscript book written by the mother of the

late Judge Bradford, of Wilmington, Delaware, is the following interesting account of some relics of Mary Dyre. Mrs. Bradford was a descendant of William, the second son of William and Mary Dyre, who went to Delaware about the time of his mother's death, and remained there. Mrs. Bradford says: "Several reliques of Mary Dyre have been, from generation to generation, preserved by my family with pious care. Among them a dress, worked in many colored silks, with gold and silver thread, by her own hands, and worn by her at the court of England. It has been cut up into very small pieces, and distributed to different friends of the society, to which she belonged. A few remnants only of this valued garment, remain in my possession. The groundwork of this dress, was rich white satin—butterflies, flowers, grasshoppers, with other insects, were the chosen figures. The work must have been one of time, requiring much patience and perseverance. A piece of this work is now in the Philadelphia Museum. A still more valuable relique of this venerated ancestor is her bodkin, of pure gold, bearing her initials upon it—M. D. In consequence of filing, its size has diminished. These precious particles were, from time to time, presented to friends, who had them mingled with other gold for sleeve-buttons."

I have consulted many books of heraldry, and the first grant of arms to any person bearing the name of Dyer, which I have been able to find, was in 1575, undoubtedly, granted to Sir James Dyer. On the shield are three goats. The crest is a goat's head holding a rose in the mouth. Since Sir James Dyer's day, the rose has, in many instances, been discarded from the crest, and a goat's head rising out of a ducal coronet, is used by various members of the family. There are many families in England, at the present day, named Dyer, to whom arms have been granted. In most cases, the goat is an emblem, showing that there is more or less consanguinity between the families.

William Andrew Dyer, of London, a great-great-great-great-grandson of Oliver Cromwell, has for his crest a demi-lion rampant, and the motto "Chi sera, sera."

Sir Thomas Swinnerton Dyer has the goat's head in a ducal coronet and, *over* the crest, the motto in Welsh. "O'r Hen Fonedd," meaning "Of an ancient, honorable race."

After a very careful examination at the Heralds' College in London, it has been ascertained and *certified* there, that the coat of arms of William Dyre is the one depicted on the last page. The Saracen's head of the crest undoubtedly denotes that some ancestors, in olden times, have taken part in the Crusades, while the three goats of the shield, show that there is a link between William Dyer, and the family of Sir James Dyer, the distinguished jurist, son of Richard Dyer, lord of the manor of Wincanton, Somersetshire, England.

CPSIA information can be obtained
at www.ICGtesting.com
Printed in the USA
LVHW021534300423
745688LV00002B/140